The CIDER Method

A Human Resource Approach to Handling Employee Complaints

THE
GROWN CIDER APPLES

THE
C.I.D.E.R.
METHOD
COMMUNICATE · INVESTIGATE
DOCUMENT · EVALUATE · RESPOND
JON GALLOP

Kendall Hunt
publishing company

Kendall Hunt
publishing company

www.kendallhunt.com
Send all inquiries to:
4050 Westmark Drive
Dubuque, IA 52004-1840

Copyright © 2019 by Jon Gallop

ISBN 978-1-7924-5269-7

Published in the United States of America

Contents

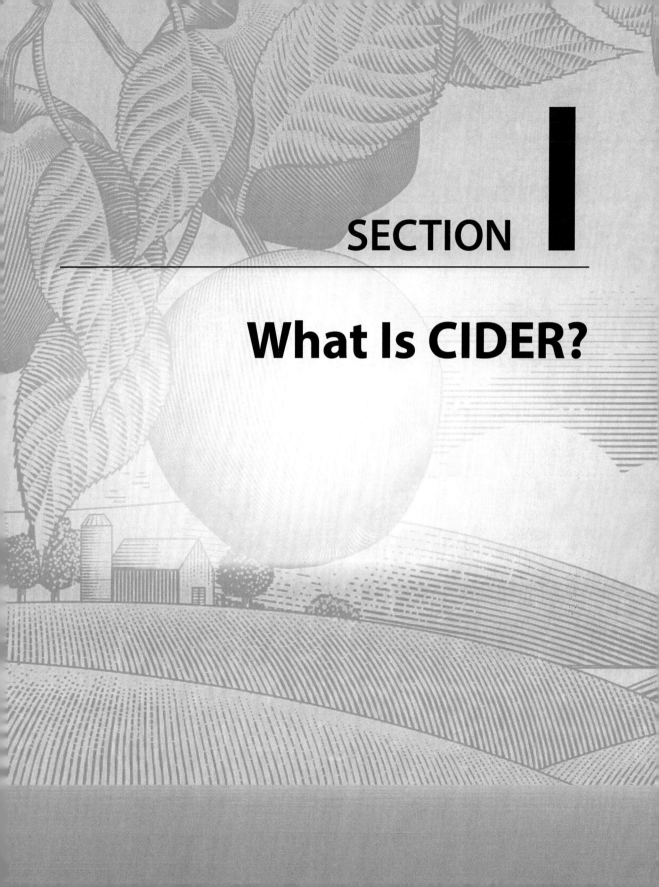

SECTION I

What Is CIDER?

CHAPTER 1

CIDER; Refined and Defined

In this age of carefully scrutinizing employer behavior, neither society nor the courts will tolerate a company that allows a toxic environment to exist by failing to properly respond to employee complaints. Mistakes made by human resource and personnel managers will be exposed and magnified when the employee hires an experienced attorney to pursue an employment law case.

There will be errors, lapses, and inappropriate behavior by individuals; however, businesses must not allow problems to continue without a systematic method for immediately identifying and rectifying these issues.

The appropriate employer response is imperative, both to protect a company from lawsuits, and on an ethical level to make the environment a better place to work. This book outlines and explains an effective and legally responsible method for undertaking an investigation to appropriately address all employee complaints and respond efficiently.

Too often companies do not properly recognize their responsibilities when faced with an employee complaint such as, "I was walking past Bill's computer and there was a group watching some video playing with like five naked people having sex on a copy machine." The supervisor says things like, "If I were you, I wouldn't walk by Bill's computer on Sexy Thursday, but I'll tell him and his cronies to turn the screen a bit more inward." Or, "Bill knows he shouldn't be doing personal stuff during company time, he better have been on his break."

Before we examine how to properly deal with Bill and the gang, the initial issue is making sure all employees are aware of how to bring their complaint(s) to

© Mike Flippo/Shutterstock.com

the attention of the employer. Consequently, it is imperative that the employer disseminates to all employees a well-written procedure for making complaints. The company's policy must elaborate the process for employees to file a grievance, and that process must be clearly outlined both during staff meetings and in the office manual.

Continuous communication between the employer and employees is the cornerstone to preventing potential workplace problems. Employers must aggressively teach employees to recognize sexual harassment, racial, religious, and age discrimination, and all other conduct that is actionable. There is no question that utilizing this proactive approach will lessen inappropriate behavior and improve the workplace environment, yet there still will be complaints.

The following chapters emphasize the necessary steps that must be employed for responding to any and all complaints. The systematic method cannot be utilized periodically or only when the issue raised is deemed serious but for every concern that is brought forward. A company cannot recognize the full extent of the problem and respond accordingly until all aspects of a complaint are understood.

Before outlining what should be done in an investigation, it is important to understand what should not be done—retaliation. An employer, who penalizes an employee for reporting violations, from discrimination based on national origin to sexual harassment, is immeasurably compounding the problem.

Firing someone for making a complaint is obvious retaliation. The more common form of this poor decision-making occurs when an employer makes the employee's working conditions harder. The courts look very closely at all actions that may rise due to retaliation, often resulting in graver consequences for the employer than the harassment itself. Managers and owners occasionally feel anger or even betrayal when a complaint is made but must swallow that inclination and make sure no employment decision is based predominantly on emotion.

Employers are usually aware that they should not simply ignore employee complaints, but the problem is their good intentions do not translate to a proper investigation. Too many companies do not have a well-defined policy in place detailing how each complaint should be handled.

This procedure cannot be a shoot from the hip, let's see what sticks process but must be a method that follows a set of guidelines to ensure a complete investigation and response. Once a concern or complaint is brought to the company's attention, a timely and comprehensive investigation is necessary.

The key to successfully handling all complaints lies in using exactly the same procedure. Think CIDER: Communicate, Investigate, Document, Evaluate, and Respond. The CIDER method evidences that the company takes each complaint seriously, makes a sincere effort to investigate the matter in a timely manner, and responds to the inappropriate conduct.

Let's examine some of the ways personnel directors and supervisors, though well intended, erroneously handle employee complaints.

Debbie reports to her supervisor that her coworker, Bob, told her he has a ranking system for women's sweaters from "frigid" to "hot," and today he told her that her sweater is off the charts based on its revealing nature and tightness. Debbie goes on to say Bob told her he had to create a whole new category for her entitled, "Whoa! It's so super-hot and sexy. Call the fire department."

The problems intensify when there is no specific policy or person to initiate the process. A manager will handle the complaint in a manner he or she deems appropriate, and often that way is erroneous, simplistic, idiotic, or all three.

The approach will range from a promise that he or she will fix everything, to saying, "Everyone loves Bob, he's a funny guy, and he did remove the Sexy Skirt-O-Meter he used to keep on his desk, so he is trying."

Debbie is on the verge of tears, so the supervisor takes a deep breath and says, "Fine, I can talk to Bob to let him know to take it down a notch." Or the supervisor will simply nod a lot and think to himself that Debbie is far too thin-skinned and will say, "C'mon he's been ranking sweaters for years and no one has minded. Tough it up."

The company may even get lucky and have a supervisor who gets it and would say to Debbie, "You shouldn't have to

© Andrii Symonenko/Shutterstock.com

Bob's Sexy Skirt-O-Meter

hear comments like that. I will fix this." But this well-meaning supervisor has no protocol to follow and will make no effort to uncover similar issues occurring in the company. In addition, he will not make a clear record of the issues for personnel files, precluding future review of what occurred and how the company responded.

Without a predetermined method in place, the handling of the complaint is dependent on the bent of the supervisor who does the initial intake. The complaining employee may have a great deal to say, but the supervisor may not take the appropriate amount of time or might simply lack patience, and much of the story will be undiscovered. To top it off, the goal of the process may be misunderstood by the person receiving the complaint, who might believe he or she should better just smooth things over or cover someone's butt.

That sound you hear is HR directors across the country weeping for all the employers who are just winging it and hoping everything will be okay. If a company has the CIDER method ready to go whenever an employee complaint is brought forward, the process will have direction, purpose, and consistency.

Another important element of having a system in place is that it proves the company is taking all complaints seriously. When employees realize that the employer is willing to give more than cursory lip service to investigating grievances, they will be far less likely to take their complaints outside the company to lawyers, newspapers, social media, and administrative agencies. If employees are satisfied that the employer is responsive to their criticism, the company will have an opportunity to remedy the situation before the issue(s) intensify to a level that makes the workplace toxic and ripe for successful employee lawsuits.

The CIDER method is easily integrated into the corporate policy. It is important that the process be a part of the company's fabric. Each business will determine if it will select an employee in-house to train or make a new hire for this position. Depending on the size of the company, the investigator's position may not be full-time, and the job description will entail other duties, but he or she must be available for immediate intake of any new complaints.

The supervisor of this process must be selected carefully because not only will they be privy to each determination, but they will also coordinate the many facets of the investigation. In addition, the supervisor is responsible for reaching a conclusion and directing the company's response to the transgression(s).

It is necessary to draft the company's office manual to include information on alerting the company to any and all grievances. The employer must also schedule meetings to make all staff aware of the proactive approach the company has adopted for handling all employee complaints. The business should be able to document that all employees and supervisors are aware of the policy for reporting complaints. The company's policies must stress zero tolerance for any harassment.

It is almost legend that companies have had supervisors try to dissuade employees from filing complaints. Alisha says, "I can't take all the constant sexual remarks from Owen. I am bringing his actions to the attention of the company." The supervisor says, "Maybe you don't want to file an official report because then there is so much paperwork and red tape. You letting me know today is good enough," . . . except for one thing . . . it is not good enough.

This book is divided into three separate sections. Chapters One to Seven detail the specific components of the CIDER method to outline the purpose, intent, and necessity of each element. Chapters Eight to Sixteen review the applicable laws that are relevant to employment situations and are necessary to properly analyze employee complaints. Chapters Seventeen to Twenty-three set forth numerous scenarios that teach the application of the CIDER method and demonstrate how to properly handle worker grievances, along with additional scenarios to apply the newfound skills.

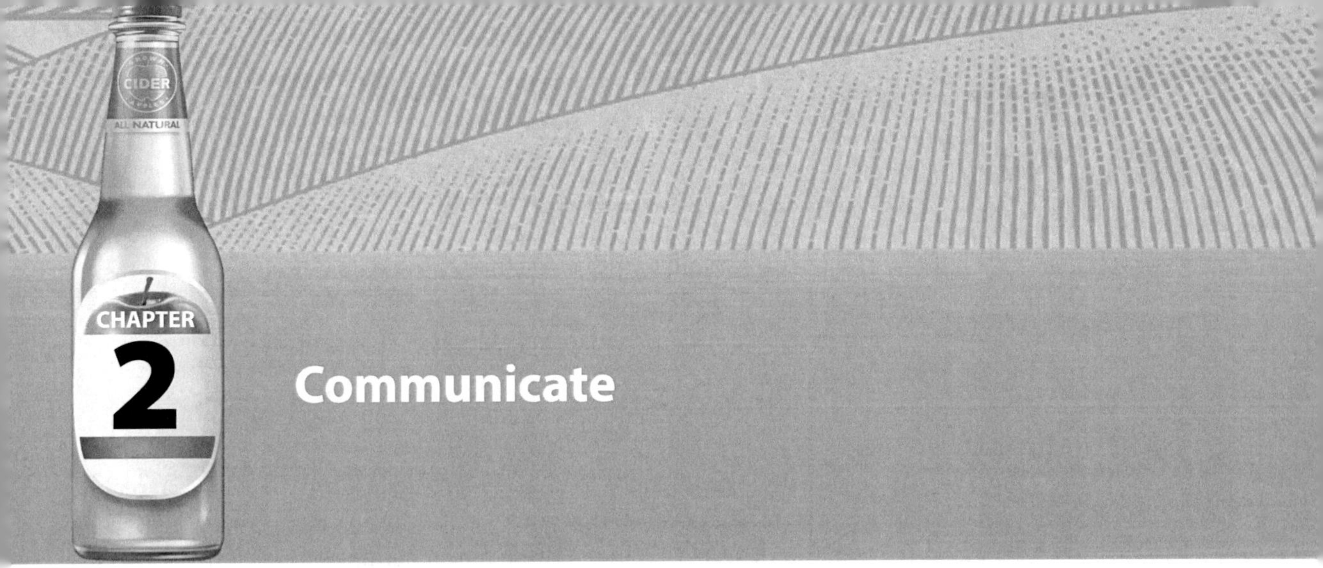

CHAPTER 2 Communicate

Communication is the first step of the CIDER method. It is the key to understanding what is happening but is often greatly misunderstood. Communicating is not about talking, it is about listening. If the company is not fully aware of the full essence of the employee complaint, the rest of the process will fall flat.

When someone complains that a person is a lousy communicator, they rarely mean the individual cannot drone on with the best of them. They are referring to the fact that the person is not paying attention to them.

> *The single biggest problem with communication is the illusion it has taken place.*
>
> *—George Bernard Shaw*

The best communication is about hearing and understanding someone else's perspectives.

Just like if Darth Vader were teaching a class on ethics—sometimes it is illuminating to see the dark side of subjects to better understand what not to do before outlining the proper approach. In that vein, let's examine Ariana's meeting with Brent, the company's intake person for employees to file complaints.

Ariana: "I am so upset about what just happened. It was horrible. I never thought this would happen to me. I feel degraded and like my value as a person was just downsized."

Brent: "This is not the best time. I am really trying to get ready for tonight's fantasy football draft. Can't it wait until tomorrow, or even better, next week?"

Ariana: "Well . . . I thought it was company policy to encourage us to come forward right away with these types of concerns."

Brent: "Fine. But just between you and me, the policy is more like bendable guidelines than hard and fast rules. So, what is bugging you today?"

Ariana: "So, my manager, Pete, asks me to come in to his . . . aren't you gonna take notes or record my concerns?"

Brent: "Not really necessary. I am more of a bottom line, main point guy. I have a pretty good memory, Alice"

Ariana: "It's Ariana. Oh . . . okay. Well as I was saying, Pete asks me to come in to his office. I go in and sit down. I assume he wants to . . . Brent? Brent?"

"Oh my goodness! You gotta see this cat video my daughter just sent me," Brent says turning his phone toward Ariana.

Ariana: "You want me to watch a cat video?! I really am not in the mood right now. I am so upset about Pete."

Brent: "But the cat is actually typing on a real keyboard to a Cardi B song. A real keyboard—hysterical! I think this would turn your whole day around. But ok, ok, let's keep going on this complaint-fest. You were telling me something about Phil or Phil's office or . . ."

Ariana: "Pete, not Phil, Pete. So, I sit down and Pete gets up and closes the door. I figure I am in real trouble. And he tells me that his wife is out of town for a week. And he can't imagine a better use of his time than starting with kissing my toes and working his way up until we are both in heaven."

Brent: "And?"

Ariana: "And what?"

Brent: "Is that your complaint?!"

Ariana: "Yes, that is my complaint! It is disgusting, upsetting, and way out of line."

Brent: "You don't have to bite my head off. Wait, is this a hormonal thing? As an aside you can take this as a compliment. I mean Pete's wife is hot with a capital H."

Ariana: "A compliment? I can't stop shaking. Pete is giving me a salary review in one week, I have my annual reports due tomorrow and . . ."

Brent: "I get it. I get it. What I hear you saying is that his being married makes this a problem."

Ariana: "No, that is hardly the issue. I am . . . are you watching another cat video? Look this is the worst day I can imagine. I come to work and my boss hits on me . . . and . . ."

Brent: "I said I get it. Life is hard. You are bothered. Look I will poke around a bit and let Pete know that you are not interested. In the meantime, I am sending you this other cat video. It will take your mind off Pete."

The first meeting with the complainant sets the tone for the entire process. It is imperative that the person designated by the company to perform the initial intake be educated to meet a high standard of great communication. Brent has clearly not been instructed properly, and he is definitely not the type of person who should be assigned this important position. Later in this chapter we will expand on the desirable attributes for personnel who will be part of the CIDER process.

The CIDER method must be integrated into an employer's policy to immediately react when an employee brings any grievance to the company's attention. Each worker within the company must be informed and educated in his or her right to make the company aware of any complaint.

It is crucial that businesses emphasize that when employees believe there is a perceived injustice, they are encouraged to immediately report their concern without any worry of employer retaliation. The company will designate staff members with the responsibility of meeting with the complaining staff member. It is imperative that there is no unreasonable delay in meeting with the employee.

Once a worker has filed or voiced his or her complaint, the individual assigned to investigate all grievances must schedule a meeting with the employee who raised the complaint as soon as possible, preferably within one business day. In the event the complaining employee is the cause for the delay in scheduling a meeting, that information must be documented with a written memo to that employee to avoid a future claim of unreasonable delay.

In addition, the company's procedure must have a backup plan in place for an alternative person to commence the investigation in the event of conflicting circumstances such as: the primary investigator having a personal relationship with one of the individuals who may be part of the investigation; the complaint centering on the primary investigator; the primary investigator being on vacation or out sick; the person making a complaint being uncomfortable discussing the issue(s) with the primary person; or any other reason that makes the primary investigator inappropriate for the role.

The initial conference should be at a place and time when the investigator is not rushed or interrupted. The goal of this meeting is to make sure the complaining employee feels the company's designated representative is extremely receptive. No judgmental comments or body language should occur in response to the employee's communication since that will often stifle his or her willingness to talk openly.

The first meeting with an employee making a complaint is perhaps its best chance for an employer to glean information. Once an investigation commences, the employee may have contacted an attorney or outside agency, which may impede the employer's ability to gather subsequent information from the employee. Consequently, this first interview being conducted properly is crucial to the success of the entire process.

Far too many people view listening as being forced to wait their turn until they can speak. They are most interested in the rebuttal as opposed to really concentrating on what is being said. We are all too familiar with friends who clearly are not listening but just waiting for you to stop talking so they can make their point. The art of truly listening is often a lost or at least a misplaced art.

An important attribute in this role is being able to patiently allow a story to unfold. The person outlining the complaint may take many side roads to get to the heart of the grievance, but if those ancillary matters are skipped over to get to the meat of the subject, other issues may be missed.

It is a great skill to make the employee feel comfortable in telling the entire story. Listening with interest is crucial for catching the nuances that may be missed due to a lack of concentration. The person conducting the interviews should be well versed in obtaining information without inhibiting the employee in any way. A good way to help refine interrogation skills is to record mock interviews. The camera should be focused on the interviewer to capture the body language and performance. The technique and style of the interviewer should be analyzed and critiqued by a mentor to refine the skills.

Interviews should not seem like cross-examinations nor should they betray opinion or assessment. The best questions to ask at this point are open-ended invitations to expand such as, "What else was said?" and "What else can you tell me about this?" Inquiries that start with the word "why" tend to put people on the defensive. This first meeting is not the time for evaluations but a time to compile information by utilizing skills to flush out every aspect of the complainant's story. It is important to wait until the person has paused before asking a question, lest they lose their train of thought or feel slighted because they were interrupted.

It may be tempting to respond with some exclamation of support, disgust, or disbelief. Don't do it. If an employee (Kathy) comes into your office and says, "Jim grabbed my backside while I was walking to the copy machine," your kneejerk reaction may be to say, "That's horrible." Or in the alternative, you may want to say, "Jim's just kidding around. I tell everyone you gotta take Jimbo with a grain of salt."

These types of comments are destructive to the entire process. If the interviewer defends Jim, that will limit the complaining employee's willingness to provide details, destroying the company's ability to accumulate all the necessary information.

If the questioner takes the other approach and affirms or validates the employee's story with some pacifying or gratuitous comments on whatever story the employee is relaying, the employee will leave the office and likely tell the first person he or she sees how horrified the company is, making it appear that the objectivity is absent.

The interviewer's skills to obtain all the allegations in a neutral manner are essential to handling complaints properly. The entire responsibility at this point is to find out the complaining employee's full version of the events.

The interviewer should lean forward and make direct eye contact, because those cues are crucial in conveying interest. It is not just verbal comments that may limit this process; an employee may interpret nonverbal cues, such as eye rolling or deep breaths, as boredom or doubt. A brief glance at the phone by the person conducting the interview (like Brent with his cat videos) will disrupt the entire flow and shows a lack of commitment to the person registering the complaint.

The nonverbal cues also go the other way. What can be ascertained from observing the person making a complaint? Tone, slumping of the shoulders, and unwillingness to make eye contact can give the interviewer some additional information. Words may convey only part of the story.

Experienced HR directors keep a box of tissues on their desk, and when the person starts crying, they will push the box toward them and not take their crying as an invitation to comfort, but rather as a signal that there is far more information to be obtained.

The interview should not be over until all avenues of questioning have been exhausted. Some stories, especially in the area of sexual harassment, can be quite graphic, and a display of shock or even embarrassment may inhibit the person.

Prior to ending the meeting, the detailed notes should be read out loud to the interviewee to confirm that they are 100% accurate. The meeting should not end until the interviewer is convinced that there are no other issues, concerns, or ancillary matters left uncovered. The notes should be typed, and a signature of the employee obtained to confirm their accuracy and that the employee has no additional complaints.

In addition to creating a detailed official report of the interviewee's version of the situation, the interviewer must make personal notes on their own assessment of credibility and any other factors that will help them remember the essence of that interview. The interviewer will use the unofficial notes when discussing the complaint during the evaluation phase. These personal impressions will be invaluable in jogging their memory after they interviewing numerous witnesses. The unofficial notes will not be part of the file, rather, are for the interviewer's use to enhance their contribution to the evaluation.

Each time a staff member files a complaint, the story of how the company reacted to the complainant will circulate among the staff. This word of mouth is critical for employees to understand all complaints are taken seriously not just because it was stressed at a meeting, but in reality. The complaining worker will either tell how they were encouraged to outline their story including depth and details without being rushed or that they were not taken seriously and the employer clearly does not care. Consequently, the employee assigned to obtain the initial report of problems sets the tone for the company.

Occasionally an employee will voice a nebulous complaint such as, "There is some really bad sexual harassment going on at the company, but I don't really want to make an official complaint. I just thought you should know. I'll give you specifics if you promise to keep everything confidential and not do anything official." That is a very serious predicament.

Do not under any circumstance make a promise to keep this or any similar issue confidential. Once the company has knowledge of a concern, it must be addressed and acted on with the CIDER method. It does not matter that the employee is embarrassed or is telling you as a friend or does not want to cause trouble; the company, once aware, must act swiftly.

The problem is that the business is now aware something is going on, and yet the person who has the details will not agree to disclose the specifics without an agreement that the employer will not pursue the matter. This is like someone going to the police station and saying "I know a bomb is planted somewhere, and it is going to go off at some point, but I won't tell you anything else unless you agree not to try and find or disarm the bomb." Not a healthy situation.

Consequently, it is imperative to convince the person to divulge what they know for the good of the other employees, the company, and the work environment. Many individuals who preface their conference with that request are often anxious to set forth all that they know, but hold back because they worry about being labeled a snitch.

It is critically important that you help the person realize that they are helping make the workplace better, and it is likely that by not reporting the activity it is adversely affecting other employees. Convince them of the company goal to stop any inappropriate behavior. Keep working on the employee to assure them that the person who brings the complaint forward is in no danger of retribution. Be persistent in showing how important it is to the company to be made aware of any questionable conduct not to punish but to remedy.

In the event the person cannot be convinced to reveal their story, the company must be able to prove that they tried to elicit the information. Further, a supervisor must be brought in and made aware of the circumstances. The supervisor or the owner of the company should meet with the employee to try a different approach to elicit the employee's concerns. The employer should not give up until all reasonable efforts are exhausted to obtain the information.

As with all aspects of the method, all attempts and efforts must be documented including the reticence of the employee in question.

The communication step of the CIDER method cannot be handled in a haphazard manner with someone who is untrained, insensitive, or obtuse. The company must select this person for the position with care and train them properly. Hearing is a physical trait, but listening is a skill that must be cultivated and valued in this position. Effective communication is the key. Without good communication the thrust of a complaint or underlying message may be missed.

Displaying interest and asking pertinent open-ended questions to facilitate the process is integral to making the complaining employee feel valued. The company must help develop the listening skills among its personnel that will make for a successful first step of the CIDER method. Patience and attentiveness are key attributes in facilitating the employee's willingness to outline all of the concerns. The interview is not over if the employee has anything else to say in regard to the complaint from the day they started work to the present.

Investigate

CHAPTER 3

The first meeting between the complainant and the employee designated by the company to initiate the process is complete. The company chose wisely and has an individual who does an excellent job obtaining the full version of each complaint.

The process is now ready for the "I" in the method, and that is Investigate. The courts put the onus on the employer to conduct a thorough and proper investigation. Companies must always ask, "Do the circumstances suggest potential harassment or discrimination?" The investigation must consider both areas, no matter how subtle, and flush out all potential concerns.

The fact that a complaining employee may not outline every potential issue does not excuse an employer from failing to uncover a problem area. The company is responsible for conducting a comprehensive investigation to reveal any issues of unwelcome harassment that may be present or emerging.

The investigation may also be analyzed by looking at the dark side of things. Let's return to Brent. He finished meeting with Arianna to discuss her complaint against Pete, her supervisor, who said he wanted to start at kissing her toes and work his way up to heaven. Brent decides that he should smooth things over and just talk to Pete. He heads to Pete's office and begins.

Brent: "Petey. The Pete-ster. Doctor P. The P.-man. How's it shakin?"

Pete: "Brent, my man. Brent-a-licious."

Brent: "Got something we gotta talk about. You know Arianna?"

Pete: "Most definitely, I do. She is fine."

Brent: "She came in my office to register a complaint about you."

Pete: "Now what?"

Brent: "She says you told her your wife is out of town and that you want to start licking her toes and move up until you get to heaven."

Pete: "Guilty. A lady's man all the way. High five."

Brent: "I am gonna put down that you didn't really say that, but if you did say something along those lines, you were taken out of context."

Pete: "Works for me"

Brent walks out with satisfaction knowing that he completed the investigation, and he could get right back to preparing for his fantasy football draft. Brent was correct to meet with Pete, but outside that, nothing else about the meeting and investigation was done properly.

The best procedure for handling an investigation is to have a well-trained, intelligent employee (unlike Brent) responsible for compiling the particulars. Proper training should consist of a minimum of reputable employment seminars that are offered by most state's continuing legal education programs on an annual basis and reading this book, as well as practice interviews with the supervisor critiquing the process to refine questioning skills.

It is essential that the person assigned to conduct the investigation recognize not only the reported issues of discrimination and harassment, but also those unreported and simmering beneath the surface. They should possess an ability to investigate objectively, have no stake in the outcome, and have the proper temperament to conduct interviews.

Subsequent to the initial interview with the complaining employee, there should be a meeting between the fact finder and the supervisor to discuss and plan the overall approach for the investigation including compiling a witness list and formulating proposed interview questions. Having another experienced person's perspective to examine the problems is important to ensure a more complete investigation. The supervisor of the process should have basic knowledge of employment issues and the current state of the law. Preparation for all meetings is essential.

There are many companies that have only a few employees; consequently, it is not feasible to have one individual assigned for intake and another employee acting as the supervisor in the CIDER method. Most likely the owner of the company will be the interviewer, investigator, and evaluator. The individual responsible for handling all aspects of the complaint process should still consult with another person to obtain a separate point of view. A consultation with an employment law attorney is always an option, but the cost may be prohibitive. Other alternatives include obtaining an opinion from the Equal Employment Opportunity Commission (EEOC), consulting with their insurance carrier, talking to a representative from an employee assistance program, or speaking to an experienced colleague who can be trusted to keep matters confidential.

Personnel files of the relevant employees to the present complaint must be reviewed to determine if there are prior notations of past misconduct. Being able to utilize the reports in employee files is mandatory for recognizing patterns and potential problems.

Subsequent to hearing the employee's complaint, the plan for the investigation must be determined on a case-by-case basis after meeting with the supervisor. Often the next step of the inquiry may be to interview the employee who is the main subject of the complaint.

The interviews of employees named in the complaint, as well as witnesses, must be conducted in the thorough manner outlined in Chapter Two to properly obtain all the relevant facts and information. The meeting cannot be casual but should be professionally handled to ensure that the gravity of the process is not undermined. The interviewer's cultivated skill of listening carefully to responses will often lead to important follow-up inquiry that may reveal more problems than were brought up in the initial complaint.

It is essential that each interview begins with an explanation of the process. The interviewer should state that the company handles every complaint in the same manner. For example: "We investigate each and every concern raised by any employee. Furthermore, we have not made any determination as to the validity and accuracy of the complaint but are simply compiling information to better assess the situation."

In the example of Kathy claiming Jim inappropriately touched her, Jim will be called in to the interviewer's office. If the interviewer opens with, "Jim, an employee here is saying you grabbed her backside; why would you do that?" That interview will likely not go smoothly. It is beneficial to begin the conversation with a consistent preamble that will reduce the defensiveness such as, "Jim, as you know it is our office policy to investigate each and every complaint we receive. We have not formed any opinion regarding the merits of this complaint, and we are simply investigating this as we do with all complaints, big or small." This approach helps employees understand you are not accusing, but investigating.

Ultimately, you will get to the part where the specifics of the complaint are shared. The initial reaction of the interviewee may be anger, shock, disbelief, or somewhere in between, but an experienced interviewer will be able to defuse the emotional aspect and stick to obtaining the person's complete version of the story.

The ability to compile information in a manner that convinces a jury that the company went beyond a simplistic effort is a key aspect of the process. An investigation should prove that the goal was to discover all the perspectives, issues, and potential problems.

The investigation should be approached with the idea that whenever an employee is disciplined, they will claim the inquiry or findings were incomplete or unfair. Consequently, examine the information obtained from all points of view, especially from the perspective of the employee who is the subject of the complaint. The evidence should attempt to close off all employee claims that information supporting their side was overlooked.

The investigative process should err on the side of compiling too much material versus too little, not only to prove the employer's fact-finding was thorough, but also because additional evidence often leads to a more accurate determination.

It is similarly essential that the investigation is timely. The courts are very clear that the investigation must be conducted within a reasonable time frame (Harvill v. Westward Communications, 433 F.3d 428 [5th Cir. 2005]). An expedient investigation ensures witnesses have accurate recollection of the events as well as quickly remedying workplace issues raised by the complaint.

When the courts or the EEOC evaluate if the employer's response was timely, there is not a prescribed period of time to complete the task, such as within one week or 10 days, but time is of the essence. There is rarely a justifiable reason for an investigation taking more than a few weeks. If the investigation is put on hold, unreasonably delayed, or the ball simply dropped, and that is the employer's justification for not correcting the problem, the company will likely be found liable.

It may turn out that the complaining employee has made 17 other complaints that were investigated and determined to be unfounded. That does not mean the employer should ignore complaint number 18, but if after the company uses the CIDER method to determine that the newest filing is without merit, it may be time to consider dealing with the serial complainer.

The main goal of an investigation is to produce a reliable set of facts to reach a conclusion. An unbiased investigation will better serve a company in terms of ethics, fairness, and being able to have a sound basis for its conclusion(s).

The investigation should not be sloppy, lazy, or minimal. Plan out the process, formulate probing questions, and move quickly. The proper people should be interviewed with depth to make sure the fact-finding uncovers the essential information leading to an accurate evaluation.

Sometimes the conduct referenced in the complaint is so serious and pervasive that an interim action must be taken prior to the completion of the investigation. This is a rare occurrence, but in the case of physical assault, the safety of the employee is paramount. If the company believes that an employee should be temporarily suspended pending the compilation of all the evidence, the action must be considered carefully since that measure may convey a premature finding of misconduct in regard to the accused. Consequently, there may be other subtler interim measures that can be taken which will protect the victim until the company has accumulated enough evidence to make an accurate final evaluation.

Five samples of employee interview summaries are included at the end of Chapter Twenty-three.

Document

In our adversarial court system, verdicts are unfortunately not about truth but about proof. Consequently, cases are won and lost, not based on who is right and who is wrong, but based on documented evidence.

Without proper documentation, it is often one word against another. A typical juror tends to favor an employee over an employer (Civil Trial Cases and Verdicts in Large Counties, Carol J. DeFrances, et al., Bureau of Justice Statistics, [1999]). Retrieved from [https://www .bjs.gov/content/pub/pdf/ctcvlc96.pdf]).

It is not enough to do the right thing. The employer must be able to prove they did the right thing. Written, detailed documentation is the stuff winning verdicts are made of.

The "D" portion of the CIDER method, which stands for document, permeates each section and is paramount in not only proving an employer's defense, but also in properly handling future complaints. The best documentation is an in-depth, written account of all issues raised and discussed. Detail and specifics are keys to successful documentation.

Looking at Brent, he is a prime example of the improper approach. Brent vaguely remembers about a week after the interviews that he is supposed to document all his work so he quickly jots down the following: "Forced to have a little chat with Arianna. She perceived, perhaps mistakenly, that Pete was coming on to her (look who thinks she is all that). Met with Pete, who is a great guy. He says she misunderstood his intent." He puts that sheet of paper in the top left drawer of his desk.

The Brent approach goes against the clear mandate that the documentation of interviews should be immediate, detailed, thorough, factual, and free of any opinions, speculation, or editorial remarks. Brent misfired on all accounts.

It is not sufficient to simply take cursory notes when interviewing an employee. When preparing for trial, the lawyer handling the defense of the employer will never look back and say, "No, no, no, this is way too thorough. You have far too many details, quotes, and specifics in your memorandum."

Each step of the CIDER method must be thoroughly documented, including every meeting from the initial intake to the evaluation and response. The written record of the investigation, findings, and all pertinent information must be placed in all relevant personnel files as standard office procedure.

By the time the employee's case against the company gets to a district court trial, it may be 3 years after the complaint.

© sirtravelalot/Shutterstock.com

If detailed, well-documented notes are not created at the time of the various meetings, the person representing the company testifying at trial will have an illegible mess for notes. Their testimony in court or at a deposition will go something like this:

> *Lawyer:* "Tell me what was said by the employee during the initial meeting with you?"
> The company representative, Marlene, will be trying desperately to decipher the hand-written bullet points.
> *Marlene:* "Ms. Thomas came in, not sure what day this was, but like a Tuesday or maybe Thursday or a day ending in Y and told me something about . . . spaghetti . . . no that's not it . . . she said something about sinking a ship . . . no . . . I think she said she is behind or wants to be kind or . . ."
> *Lawyer:* "What did Ms. Thomas tell you about the encounter with her supervisor?"
> *Marlene:* "Ah, it looks like she was upended or upset or updated or up something about the way he tip-toed, no that's not it, the way he talked, no, the way he touched her lemur or lemon or leg or some L word . . ."

However, if copious notes are taken during the initial interview without shortcutting what is said, the company representative will take the stand 3 years later and be able to impress the jury with specifics and quotes. People are far more willing to give credibility to a person who can outline a 3-year-old conversation with detail and depth than to someone who stammers, paraphrases, and struggles to recall the conversation with clarity.

In addition, the employee who conducted the investigation is often no longer available. If this is the case, then the detailed notes of the intake meeting are even more valuable.

Documentation regarding all aspects of the process cannot be overemphasized. Again, it is not enough to handle situations properly; it is about proving the employer handled the situation properly. A party to a lawsuit wins a case because they have the best documented evidence, not because they did the right things.

Recording interviews is another option in addition to taking detailed notes. The upside to having meetings recorded is the lack of opportunity for the complaining employee to argue that the notes were not accurate. An audio recording can also negate an employee's claim that they did not bother to read or was pressured to sign the document. Further, a recording allows others to better assess the interviewee's credibility. The downside of recording conversations is when some employees are informed that they are being recorded, they are less willing to discuss and expand on specifics they have witnessed or believe they have witnessed.

Every step of each process must be documented without exception. Employees will come and go, but documentation will always be there to provide evidence of the incidents and responses years later.

Proper documentation of interviews means that the formalized account is comprehensive and contains exact quotes from the individual being interviewed. In addition, the written account must list the date, start and end time, the location, and list the names of all those present at the interview. A signature of the person being interviewed must be obtained to confirm and prove the accuracy of the account by the interviewee.

Documentation of conferences, such as those to plan the direction of the investigation, reach a conclusion, or move forward with the response, must outline each element of the meeting with clarity and depth to ensure there are no key aspects missing.

Examples of the summaries of meetings and interviews are set forth in the last chapter of the book.

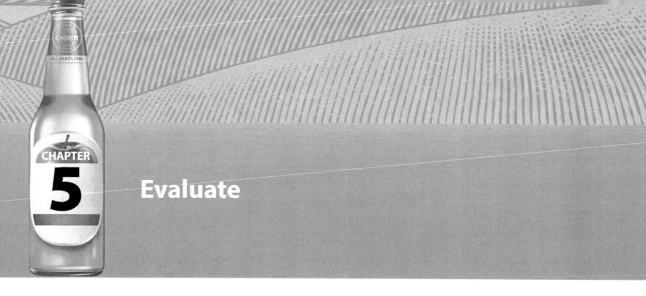

Evaluate

While no determination or even hypothesis should be part of the initial stages of compiling the information, now the time has come to make that evaluation based on the evidence obtained during the investigation.

This stage is where the people assigned with the task of reaching a conclusion must determine if the complaint was valid, or in essence, they must decide who screwed up and how serious was the screw up.

If the supervisor is convinced that all the relevant information for making an accurate evaluation is part of the file, it is time to decide. The supervisor along with the investigator should review all the compiled data. This determination is the key to the company's response and, hence, it must be considered carefully.

It is sometimes helpful to review past EEOC decisions when evaluating a workplace complaint that brings up some gray areas of the law. The EEOC is the administrative agency responsible for investigating and enforcing federal laws which make it illegal to discriminate against applicants or employees based on their protected status (protected categories will be discussed in the upcoming chapters).

In some limited situations, the employer should consult an experienced employment law attorney for specific guidance. Any legal research or communications with a lawyer or advisor should be specifically documented including names, dates, information provided to the attorney, and a detailed summary of the legal advice.

Evaluating Applicable Insurance Coverage

Insurance coverage may be a consideration in the evaluation process. If a company has purchased Employment Protection Liability Insurance (EPLI), there will be potential coverage for many employment law claims, from sexual harassment to racial discrimination. Most policies clearly set forth how coverage is triggered and consequently must be carefully reviewed.

Some EPLI coverage is triggered by an administrative complaint (such as to the EEOC), while other policy language may say the commencement of a lawsuit (serving and filing the summons and complaint) initiates coverage. Most policies state the insured must report a claim "as soon as practical." The business must make sure it does not fail to notify the insurance carrier to avoid a denial of coverage based on failure to cooperate. Consequently, the company must evaluate if this is a proper time to notify the insurance carrier.

Business owners often complain that their EPLI insurance company is too quick to settle lawsuits rather than fighting. The typical insurance policies have a clause requiring an insurance company to seek approval prior to settling, but most agreements have language stating approval from the business will not be unreasonably withheld. It is important that the employer must document all contacts with the insurance company to keep some control of the process without jeopardizing coverage. Even if a business has purchased EPLI insurance coverage, they must employ the CIDER method in addition to educating employees with regard to appropriate behavior. This limits employee issues from mushrooming into administrative complaints and lawsuits, keeps insurance rates lower, and more importantly, it fosters a high-quality work environment.

Regardless of whether there is insurance coverage, the final evaluation of every complaint must be reviewed in the context of these questions: Would this determination hold up in court based on the evidence? Would the company be comfortable defending its decision based on the investigation? Is there other relevant, available information that was not obtained?

The evaluation should be scrutinized in the same way as would an opposing lawyer whose entire purpose is to tear apart the determination as unfounded. Vet the appraisal from every possible angle. Anticipating cross-examination of the corporate executives by an experienced attorney zealously representing the employee will serve the company very well. Do not wait until 4 weeks before the case proceeds to trial to flush out all the potential problems with assessment.

A key to any aspect of business is being able to anticipate potential arguments. There is no substitute for preparation. The additional time spent at this juncture, instead of rushing to judgment, will save the company serious problems down the road.

Preparing for all possible areas of attack on the final evaluation will make sure the determination can withstand allegations of too limited investigation or failure to consider other relevant evidence.

Employers need to consider, not just how the case will be defended in court, but how the story will play out on the 6:00 p.m. local news. If the employee does not sue, but instead tries to get the attention of a reporter who likes going after employers on behalf of employees, would the business be able to justify its conclusions? The evaluation should hold up in both a court of law and in the court of public opinion.

The determination of whether there was misconduct on the part of one or more employees is the key to the final step. This must not be taken lightly, and it is imperative that the parties involved make sure there are no additional witnesses or evidence that should be considered. Employees know when a company is taking the easy road to obtain information. The depth of the process will evidence the thoroughness of the investigation, in addition to showing other personnel the company's commitment in taking each grievance seriously.

Our misguided friend, Brent, now realizes he has to reach an evaluation regarding Arianna's complaint against Pete. Brent is not concerned with having a complete unbiased investigation as the foundation to his determination. He simply wants to get this done and move on. His evaluation: "Arianna is a bit high-strung and overly sensitive to men giving her compliments. Pete was doing her a solid, and this was an isolated incident. The bottom line: no worries." If you think that Brent is single-handedly trying to plunge the company into the depths of a hostile work environment, you would be absolutely correct. But the key is learning from his errant ways.

The ultimate goal of the evaluation is to make sure the employer has examined the complaint from all points of view. The purpose of the evaluation is not to justify the predetermined, "protect the company" approach. The company's conclusion and response should improve the workplace environment and rid the employer of dangerous behavior and inappropriate conduct.

A specific and clear finding on all aspects of the decision must be outlined in detail. The report must include date and time, investigative process, rules, policies or laws in play, findings, and reasons therefore. Do not put opinions in the report that are masquerading as facts.

The written record should be organized and must outline how the company weighed the evidence and assessed the credibility of witnesses. It is essential that the evaluation addresses evidence that runs contrary to the final conclusions. The final report cannot ignore the material that does not support the findings. It must explain why each piece of evidence does not carry the weight of the other information.

The final evaluation that the company reaches will run the gamut from no improper behavior to a severe violation of company policy; it must be founded on sufficient, credible, and reliable proof.

The report must not be a quick jotting of the situation so that the company can get this thing over with. The documentation is critical to prove the employer made every effort to seek out and review all the relevant information to make a fair decision. The record should be self-contained. Consequently, the investigation summaries must be included as attachments to the final evaluation report.

A sample evaluation report is included in Chapter Twenty-three for review and guidance.

Respond

The entire process builds toward how the company will respond to the complaint. The company has the burden to prove that the response is a reasonable attempt to remedy the behavior or atmosphere.

It should be a common-sense concept that if the company has given a written warning to the same employee on five previous occasions over the past 3 years for virtually the same transgressions, the newest response of a sixth written warning is not reasonably calculated to fix the problem.

Often the transgressions are subtler. If, for example, there have been separate complaints against different employees, but the essence of the issue(s) identified is similar, the employer must recognize it needs to take swift action and initiate company-wide education to fix the problem(s).

If a jury concludes that the company is not making a real effort to remedy the hostile work environment because of an unreasonable or inappropriate response, the company will likely be writing a large check for damages.

Prior to finalizing the company's course of action, it is important to carefully scrutinize the situation including, but not limited to, past similar violations, severity of the behavior, and clear evidence of the present infraction.

The company should not threaten or warn employees without some substance to the complaint. An unsubstantiated warning, suspension, termination, or other adverse employment action could result in the alleged harasser having a viable defamation of character lawsuit (Raytheon Technical Services Inc. v. Hyland 641 S.E. 2d 84 [Va. Sup. Ct. 2007]). A finding that the investigation was too limited would lead a court to conclude that the determination was reckless, leading to an award in favor of the employee.

Even if the findings indicate no wrongful behavior occurred and that no action should be taken, documentation is still a must. The lack of a specific finding will support the company's decision for the limited action it takes.

The response may include: termination, warning, suspension, moving the employee, or sending the employee to sensitivity training. The employer may choose other possibilities ranging from no action to a more severe response. The final report must outline the alternatives considered to remedy the behavior in question stemming from the evaluation including the reasons for choosing or not choosing each option.

Firing an Employee

When the evaluator(s) finds that the best response is to fire an employee, the termination must be handled properly to avoid creating any additional problems.

Firing an employee should never be done without a witness to the process. Some discharged employees seek revenge against the employer. Suffice it to say the discharged worker will rarely have warm fuzzy feelings upon being let go. When the fired employee demands to know who ratted on him or her during the investigation, it is imperative that the employer maintain confidentiality; this will limit retaliation by the terminated employee against the witness.

If a company decides that firing is the best response, it is advisable to terminate the employee at the end of the work day whenever possible to avoid a scene. A termination checklist should be made in advance and followed to make sure all bases are covered.

When discharging the employee, do not drag out the dialogue. The person running this meeting should get to the point. It should not go like this: "So, nice weather we're having. What about those Vikings? Would you like a donut? Oh, and clear out your desk and never come back. Are those new shoes? They look great." The employee should understand this is a final decision. Do not soften the words conveying the impression that the worker could talk his or her way into a lesser punishment or could reapply later.

Once the meeting is complete and the employee has been told they are fired, make sure their access to any security or information systems, and any customer communication has been disabled. Furthermore, make an effort to minimize contact with other employees as the process of firing the employee is unfolding.

If possible, have a security officer escort the former employee out of the building. Most companies, however, do not employ security officers. Either way, you must not allow him or her to be alone in the office, and two employees should stay with the discharged employee until he or she has left the building.

The escort(s) should make sure the fired employee does not take any company property while vacating the premises. Furthermore, when he or she is going through the items that they claim are personal possessions, someone should be able to confirm the ownership of the property in question.

There are certain legal requirements that must be met when employees are terminated, such as getting them their paycheck in the statutorily mandated (very limited) amount of days and providing them with COBRA information. The employer should calculate the amount the employee is owed plus any vacation time and have the check ready to hand over as part of the termination process.

Do not ignore the situation with the other workers the next day. Address the fact that the employee is no longer with the company. Be direct to avoid confusion as to why the person is gone. When an employee is discharged it is crucial to the company morale to openly discuss the situation including who will take his or her immediate obligations. The staff should be treated with respect and dignity. Secrecy is not a good policy when it comes to employees suddenly being gone.

Warnings and Suspensions

There are many other responses short of firing someone. If the evaluator(s) determines a warning is the proper response, the written warning should be specific. The classic example of an ineffective warning is to state, "It was determined that your bad attitude is a problem, and you need to work on that immediately."

The phrase "bad attitude" is the crutch of the weak-minded and lazy employer. What does that even mean? Instead of the generic phrase that means very little, set forth the details of the company's concerns, such as, "The corporate investigation has revealed you have used the following phrases to demean and belittle your female co-workers: 'You must be having PMS. You really need to stay in the kitchen. This is why women should not be paid the same as men.'" The company's written warning would also include the ramifications of future violations along with specific goals that must be met.

The warning given to the employee must be written, not only to properly document the company's response, but also to avoid misunderstandings. The language in the warning needs to be definitive. Do not preface the warnings with a weak introduction such as, "Our investigation makes it <u>appear</u> that your <u>alleged</u> behavior is <u>not fully in line</u> with our policy . . ." The wording must be strong and clear, unlike the ambiguity created by the underlined words above.

Furthermore, it is essential the consequences of repeated violations should not be subtle or subject to interpretation. The written admonition should be in unambiguous language. It is acceptable to mention a legal conclusion such as sexual harassment, but the memo must also contain plain language such as "employee misconduct" or "violation of company policy" prominently in the written warning.

In addition to firing and warning employees, there are other appropriate company responses such as: scheduling one or a series of staff education sessions with workshops, sensitivity training directed at one employee to help them acquire the skills to make better judgements, and/or moving an employee to a different location. When choosing sensitivity training, a record must be kept documenting the process and attendance. Online training is available, but in-person seminars are superior for attendees to absorb the material and for the employer to verify attendance.

The company may also suspend employees for a period of time in response to the behavior. The suspension can be with or without pay depending on the severity of the infraction.

A suspension should have a purpose that is beyond punitive. The written documentation that is given to the employee should be instructive. The language should teach the employee by outlining the specific behavior that is at the heart of the disciplinary measure and give recommendations for fixing or improving the problems or conduct.

Employees who are suspended often quit within a short time after the suspension. If an employer believes the employee has value to the company, they should carefully consider the ramifications of a strictly punishment-oriented suspension as opposed to showing that the employee is valued but made a mistake that can be corrected with behavior modification.

If the written warning simply says, "Failure to correct the problem may result in further disciplinary action, up to and including possible termination," that language is more about expressing power and instilling fear than trying to improve the situation. That type of warning might as well say, "You have two strikes, and one more and you are out of here, so if you are so stupid that you can't see the handwriting on the proverbial wall, we are laying it out for you."

While the tagline on the warning should emphasize the seriousness of not correcting his or her actions, the language therein should clearly outline the problem to make sure the employee has full clarity as to the behavior(s) that brought him or her to this point.

It is imperative to emphasize the constant refrain of this book and that is that the employer's response must not be, or even appear to be, arbitrary or subject to an inference that the action was based on an employee's inclusion in a protected category. Consequently, if a pattern emerges that some groups within protected categories tend to be suspended while other groups of employees are only warned for similar actions, this will be found to be illegal discrimination.

Settlement

Occasionally, the company may determine that the best response is to pay off an employee and terminate the employer–employee relationship. The payment (sometimes referred to as a severance package) is made in return for the employee waiving any and all rights to potential lawsuits or claims against the company. The need for this type of a resolution is not common, but may arise when there are few other good options.

If an employee has a viable claim for sexual harassment against an owner of the business, it is not feasible to fire a primary stakeholder in the company. When an owner is the source of the problems, it is extremely complicated to address the misconduct. The human resource person confronting the owner with his or her serious breaches of protocol must use all their skills to convince the head of the company that, without a change, the business and their personal reputation will be ruined.

If the company makes a finding of inappropriate behavior against an employee who is integral to the company's success, the company may be forced into a difficult choice. While the complaining employee is innocent of any inappropriate behavior, the company may be dependent on the key employee. Consequently, when evaluating the potential responses, the financial interest may alter the outcome.

In extreme cases, the best resolution may be a payment to the aggrieved employee as consideration for them resigning from their job and executing a release waiving their rights to all potential employment claims. A Non-Disclosure Agreement (NDA) or confidentiality clause should be part of any written settlement agreement. The size of the cash settlement will depend on the severity of the infraction(s). A company will need to retain an experienced employment law attorney to handle the specifics of this severance or settlement agreement because there must be specific language to properly release the employee's right to sue for their claims including, but not limited to, age, disability, and equal pay discrimination.

There may be readers who are saying, "You mean this company is gonna keep the lousy acting employee around and then pay off and jettison the worker who did nothing wrong? That is so contrary to fairness and ethics." Sometimes the financial considerations trump normal responses. Be forewarned, however, it is likely that the key employee will cause further problems with other employees with inappropriate behavior. When word spreads that the company paid off the complaining employee, other workers may dredge up prior misconduct by that key employee toward them to initiate a new complaint. Consequently, paying off one employee will probably not be the final payout unless the inappropriate behavior is rectified.

Once the dust has settled, the company must address the employee's flaws and make sure the conduct is remedied, or the payouts will be a constant business expense. In addition, the workplace environment will deteriorate, leading to a culture that tolerates a hostile work environment. In the long run, the cost to the company may be far more than if they had just terminated the key employee.

As with all the aspects of the process, the particular response must be communicated clearly without room for interpretation or ambiguity.

Keeping Files Confidential

All warnings shall be placed in the personnel files of the affected employees. Companies should have two sets of personnel files. One set should contain general personnel information such as the job application, offer letter, salary information, and attendance. The other files should encompass the more sensitive employee materials including investigation records, I-9 forms (verifying citizenship and immigration status), and other highly confidential material that could give rise to a defamation or invasion of privacy lawsuit if such facts were discovered by others within the company.

It is also important that employees are secure that the information they give as part of a company investigation will be held confidentially. The point is, make sure only designated employees have access to the separated confidential files with very strong passwords and a firewall to avoid a clever employee from hacking into the electronic files.

The next line may cause a few readers to roll their eyes and yell, "C'mon grandpa get out of the 90s," but some businesses still use real file cabinets. If that is the case, make sure they are well constructed and virtually impossible to break into to save the additional defense fees from defamation lawsuits when the sensitive information is circulated to other people.

An employer's response to a complaint should be fair and reasonable and based on a complete investigation, whether the remedy

© Lolostock/Shutterstock.com

is a training session, warning, suspension, or dismissal. The response, however, can never be based on an employee's inclusion in a protected category, or it will be considered illegal discrimination.

Follow-Up

As Yogi Berra used to say, "It ain't over till it's over." It is crucial to understand that the process is not complete just because the company responded to the behavior stemming from the complaint. The CIDER method is really C.I.D.E.R.–F.U. The F.U. of course stands for follow-up which is all too often overlooked. The company must recontact the employee in question to make sure the issue(s) is remedied or has not resurfaced and no new problems have arisen since the complaint.

An employer cannot be so arrogant as to think that their fix was perfect and ignore the issue as the months pass by. It is imperative to check back with the complaining employee in a reasonable time frame of between 2 weeks and 3 months depending on the severity of the complaint and findings.

The follow-up must not be casual but should be a formal meeting that is specifically documented. The interviewer who is assigned to revisit the matter should be familiar with the entire complaint, investigation, and response. An inquiry is necessary to make sure the behavior in question has stopped or that no new similar issues have arisen. In the event there are concerns outlined by the employee, the investigation needs to be immediately reopened and pursued with the CIDER method.

The meeting needs to review the issues that were the subject of the original complaint, and the interviewer must ask pointed questions to confirm that the problems no longer exist. It is the job of the examiner to make sure there is nothing holding the person back from saying what is on their mind. Some employees may seem hesitant to discuss current problems or they just do not want to go through the process again.

This is a dangerous situation because, if the concerns have not been resolved by the company's response, this must be uncovered. Just because the employee did not follow the recommendation of the company to report any additional problems does not mean they do not exist. The employee who filed the original complaint may think the company is monitoring the situation and is aware of any similar trouble, or in the alternative, the employee may feel the next step is to contact an employment law attorney to commence a lawsuit.

The follow-up meeting demonstrates the employer is not just doing the minimum, but cares about remedying the issues and about making sure the working environment is optimum. The formal notes outlining the employee conference must be placed in all applicable personnel files. Ongoing monitoring of each situation is integral to the process; a follow-up to the follow-up, so to speak.

A properly done reexamination with the complainant should determine if the conduct in question has stopped and should make sure no retaliation against the person who reported the behavior has taken place. Occasionally, the complainant will express dissatisfaction that more punishment was not doled out to the accused. It must be clearly emphasized that the company took the complaint very seriously and that a record of the allegation will be placed in the accused's personnel file to help keep track of future concerns.

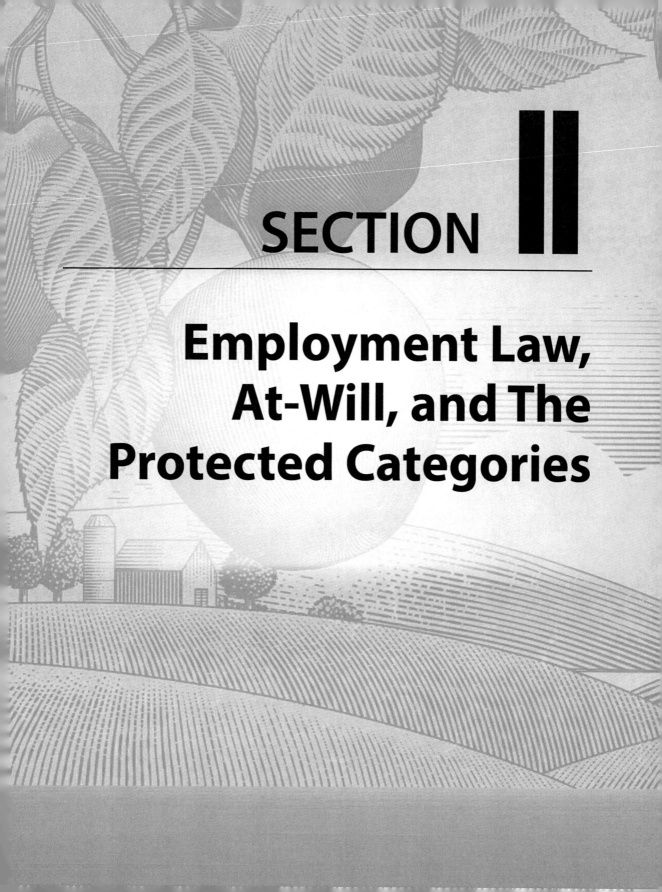

SECTION II

Employment Law, At-Will, and The Protected Categories

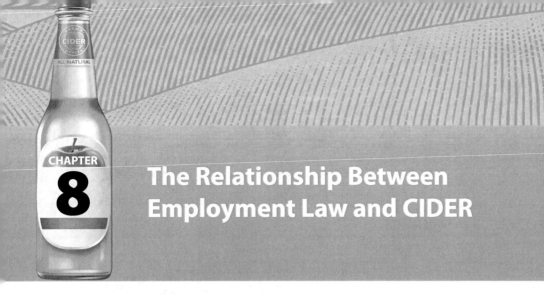

The Relationship Between Employment Law and CIDER

CHAPTER 8

In order for companies to effectively employ the CIDER method, each person involved in the process must have a working knowledge of the basics of employment law. An understanding of legal precedents and statutes allows the designated individuals to be able to spot red flags such as harassment and discrimination.

The next chapters will flush out key issues that need to be understood and addressed by companies to ensure the work environment is attractive to high-quality employees and instills pride among personnel. In addition, when a grievance is brought to the attention of the business, the underlying concerns will be recognized from all perspectives and not ignored because of a failure to identify the problems.

Truly understanding employment law enables individuals to analyze a complaint with the depth necessary to meet the high standards for properly deciding the course and scope of investigations. Being armed with the greater legal knowledge allows the employees involved in the CIDER method to accurately assess and evaluate the violations and prepare a reasonable response.

Without a solid foundation of legal knowledge, the parties involved in the process may be limited in their abilities to see all the potential land mines and thus could inadvertently sweep some serious problems under the carpet. Those problems will likely not remain hidden. Instead they could result in a finding that the company failed to recognize areas of discrimination leading to payment of damage awards in addition to an unhealthy work environment.

At-Will Employment

All employees are "At-Will" employees unless they are under contract. A union employee works under a contract, and a small minority of employees have employment contracts. Every other employee is At-Will.

The misconception that there must be reasonable cause to fire an employee is prevalent. Many in our society are convinced that an employer is unable to discharge an employee unless they have "reason-able grounds" for the employment action. However, very few have a problem understanding the At-Will concept from the other side of the aisle.

An employee walks into the boss's office and says, "I am out of here. I am gone, and you know what, I'm not giving you any reason. See ya, don't wanna be ya," then turns around and walks out, effectively quitting with zero notice.

People do not exclaim, "Hey, they can't do that! They need to have rea-sonable grounds to . . . quit."

The public seems to realize that an employee can leave his or her job without any reason. But what must be understood is that At-Will employment status applies in both directions. If an employee can quit with no notice and for no reason, the employer can fire the worker with no notice and for no reason. That is the heart of At-Will employment.

Can a boss fire a worker for wearing an ugly shirt without laying the groundwork for a great employment law case? Or because the staffer sings Celine Dion? How about because the boss is in a bad mood and fires the first person she sees? The answer is yes. An employer does NOT need reasonable cause to discharge an At-Will employee.

That means an At-Will employee can quit with no notice and for no valid reason, and conversely an employer can demote, transfer, fire, or take any employment action without notice or cause.

Question: "Is it illegal for employers to discriminate in hiring?" Most people will answer, "No, employers definitely can't discriminate." But is that accurate?

Can an employer refuse to hire someone because they have a criminal record? What about not promoting someone who has tattoos? Some will say refusing to hire or promote employ-ees with those traits is illegal because neither tattoos nor criminal records have anything to do with performing the essential duties of the job.

The belief that all discrimination is illegal is another great misconception. The reality is an employer can legally discriminate . . . with one exception. No tangible employment action may be taken if that action is based on the person's inclusion in a protected category.

The doctrine of At-Will employment makes it clear that the employer can get rid of an employee for any reason, including a bad reason, unless that reason is based on the employ-ee's inclusion in one of the protected categories.

Protected Categories

The original protected categories are:

- Sex (Gender)
- National Origin
- Religion
- Race
- Color

The five protected categories in the preceding list came first as part of Title VII of the Civil Rights Act of 1964 (Pub. L. No. 88–352, 78 Stat. 241, enacted July 2, 1964) which specifically states in part:

> *It shall be an unlawful employment practice for an employer -*
>
> *(1) to fail or refuse to hire or to discharge any individual, or otherwise to discriminate against any individual with respect to his compensation, terms, conditions, or privileges of employment, because of such individual's race, color, religion, sex, or national origin; or*
>
> *(2) to limit, segregate, or classify his employees or applicants for employment in any way which would deprive or tend to deprive any individual of employment opportunities or otherwise adversely affect his status as an employee because of such individual's race, color, religion, sex, or national origin.*

Subsequently, the United States Congress added two additional protected categories:

- Age per The Age Discrimination in Employment Act of 1967 (29 U.S.C. § 621 to 29 U.S.C. § 634) also known as the ADEA; and
- Disability per The Americans with Disabilities Act of 1990 (42 U.S.C. § 12101) also known as the ADA.

In addition, **sexual orientation** was added as a protected category based on the US Supreme Court Decision from June of 2020 in the case of Bostock v Clayton County Georgia. This category will be discussed in greater detail in Chapter Fifteen.

Also, a person who is a **whistle blower** (an employee who reports inappropriate or unethical behavior that he or she discovers at work) has some limited protection. It is considered retaliation to fire a worker who reports an issue. Consequently, a company must be able to document that its negative employment action toward that worker is unrelated to an employee filing a complaint.

In addition, there are also some **public policy** protections. An employer cannot legally fire someone for performing jury duty, voting, filing a worker's compensation claim, reporting a violation of the law or joining the National Guard, among others.

Discrimination by an employer is illegal if their decision-making is based on an employee or applicant's inclusion in a protected category. That does not mean the police will arrest the owner and charge them with a crime. It does mean, however, that the company will be subject to penalties when a government agency (such as the Equal Employment Opportunity Commission [EEOC]) finds that the business has engaged in a pattern or practice of illegal discrimination. The monetary amounts assessed against the employer may include punitive damages to punish the employer, as well as amounts constituting the complaining employee's past and future lost wages, attorney fees, and compensatory damages.

The fines levied by the administrative agency responsible for enforcing these laws are not the exclusive remedy. In addition, the employee has the right to sue the employer in civil court for their damages based on the negative employment action stemming from the illegal discrimination. A finding by the EEOC that a company illegally discriminated may be used as evidence in a civil case against the employer.

When an individual alleges that the negative employment action was based on their inclusion in a protected category, the burden shifts to the employer to prove the employment action (hiring-firing-promoting-demoting-new office-better chair etc.) was not based on the employee's inclusion in one of the protected categories.

The key in companies meeting their burden of proof is not just following legal and proper procedure, but being able to present concrete evidence, that is, documentation, to establish their defense. It is not sufficient to say, "No we did not fire Patrick because he was Irish (National Origin), we fired him because he has a bad attitude." That defense is weak and will not hold up under cross-examination. The personnel file will need to have specifics allowing a jury or judge to reach a conclusion that the employee's discharge had nothing to do with the worker's protected category status.

Hostile Work Environment

The mistaken idea that this phrase means the work environment is hostile causes a great deal of confusion. A hostile work environment is when someone is treated unfavorably because of his or her inclusion in a protected category.

A man (Steven) calls a lawyer and says, "I am pretty sure I have a slam dunk, no doubt about it, hostile work environment case."

The lawyer who hears this erroneous claim on a regular basis says, "Tell me what happened."

"I was in our weekly staff meeting yesterday. After everyone was seated, my boss, Stacy, walks to the front of the room. Everyone gets quiet and when she has everyone's attention she announces that it is time to stop the madness. She then pauses and with a grand gesture pulls out the three-page report I had turned in the day before. She shakes the papers and then holds them high above her head.

"At this point Stacy leans in to the microphone and says, 'Steven Townes, as the author of this report, please stand up so everyone can see you clearly.'

"The crowd of employees started chanting my name and I have no choice but to get up. Once I am standing she announced that the report I had submitted was the worst piece of garbage she has seen since she vomited bad fish thirteen years ago.

"She then ordered me to come to the podium, and, in front of all 85 employees, says it is her obligation as the boss, mentor, and teacher to let the entire staff know how horrible my work is.

"She waved my report at the crowd and then in my face. She begins literally ripping my report apart, page by page until the report is at least 20 pieces. She took each of the pieces and placed them on my head. She proceeded to state that I had to walk back to my seat with the shredded paper from the report on top of my scalp to remind the rest of the staff what a horrible employee I am.

© Fun Way Illustration/Shutterstock.com

"As I was walking back to my seat, Stacy said she should call the police and have me arrested since I was in essence stealing the company's money by taking a paycheck for turning in trash like the report that I was wearing as my hat of shame. It was so embarrassing, and I wanted to crawl in a hole and die. So, I want to sue my boss and the whole company for hostile work environment."

Steven believes, incorrectly, that he has a hostile work environment lawsuit based on the fact that it is, indeed, a work environment and his boss, Stacy, was clearly hostile.

This boss (Stacy the Shredder) is without a doubt a first-class jerk. But do her actions give rise to a viable civil lawsuit?

Here is the thing . . . as long as Stacy is an equal opportunity jerk, there is no problem. If, however, it can be shown that the boss only bullies certain protected groups, for example, women, Catholics or people from Denmark, then Stacy's actions are an entirely different matter and actionable. But if a boss can prove she is a jerk equally to all races, national origins, genders, colors, religions, and so on, there is no viable employment case.

If the attorney decides to take this case to trial, the employer's defense would be to march employee after employee to the witness stand to testify that the boss was incredibly rude to them. Each employee called on to testify would represent a different protected category to prove "rude but equal" treatment. The message the company would present in defense of the claim would be that the boss, Stacy, is a total egotistical maniac, but she does not differentiate on the basis of any protected category, rather, she is equally horrible to all.

Steven is not forced to work there. He can quit or he can continue to work for Stacy, but as far as a good hostile work environment case is concerned, not so much. While it is poor leadership and not great for employee morale for the boss to be a jerk, it is not actionable.

When a boss ignores one employee or favors another, this is not a violation unless an employee can prove it is more likely than not that the actions are based on the employee's inclusion in one of the protected categories. When employees are treated differently because of their status in one of the protected categories, it gives rise to a viable hostile work environment claim. There are also typically components of unwelcome behavior and more than just teasing or simply an isolated incident; but there must be discrimination based on the protected status to be accurately termed a hostile work environment.

Everyone Is In at Least Five Protected Categories

Employment law attorneys often field phone calls from owners of businesses who are nervous about disciplining one of their workers in a protected category.

"Yeah, I got this worker who is just the worst employee ever. I mean like he is so bad it is scary. I want to get rid of him, but he is some minority like Hispanic or Filipino or maybe Native American, so I am a bit worried cuz he is probably protected."

The lawyer wants to scream, "Idiot, everyone is protected!" But since the owner is paying the attorney well for the advice, the attorney would take the time to explain the concept of protected class.

The point is that every single person is in at least five protected categories. Everyone has a color, everyone has a national origin, everyone has a race, a gender, and a religion. Consequently, for employers to only think in terms of minorities as falling within protected categories misses the point.

It is an illegal firing if an employer discharges an employee for being white or male, hardly minorities. Those categories, color and gender, are protected. Consequently, if the employment action is based on inclusion in a protected category, even if the person is a nonminority within the category, that is illegal discrimination.

And That is How We Roll

An employer need not have reasonable grounds for discharging At-Will workers. However, the scenario below may help employers think a bit harder before firing a staff member for no reason.

A manager of a large company loves his absolute power. He makes employment decisions with little rhyme or reason. While that is not exactly great office policy, it is not illegal.

One morning before work he is walking in the office parking lot and steps right in some dog poop. He is angry and wants retribution, so he decides he is going to fire the first worker he sees. As he enters the front door, he sees Edwardo, a staff member and says, "Good morning. Edwardo. Is that a new shirt? I like it. And oh, by the way, clean out your desk because as of this moment you are fired."

The real problem in that situation surfaces when Edwardo sues the company and claims the termination was as a result of his inclusion in a protected category. The case heads to trial and the company's defense is on thin ice.

The cross-examination of the supervisor who fired Edwardo will proceed along these lines.

"You are Edwardo's supervisor is that correct?"

"Yes."

"And Edwardo has worked for the company for four years without any warnings or disciplinary actions, is that accurate?"

"Yes."

"Edwardo claims you fired him because he is Hispanic. You have said that is not true. Tell the court why you did fire him."

"Well . . . you probably have heard I'm a maverick, a wild card, and I believe a sudden firing sends a message to the staff."

"What is that message?"

"That you better be on your guard and working at 110% because your job can disappear at any moment. Plus, it makes sure they know who their daddy is. And that, my friend, is how we roll at J&K Enterprises."

"So, your reason for firing Edwardo is . . . no reason?"

"In a manner of speaking . . . okay, truth be told, I stepped in some doggie do-do, and it was really Edwardo's misfortune of being the first employee I saw so I had no choice. I don't make the rules, I just enforce them."

"What rules?"

"That I am an unpredictable wild card boss. One day I bring them pizza and another they are out of a job. The lesson we can all learn, my friend, is life is not always fair."

No, the real lesson learned is that the jury will not be fond of this person or company and will search for a way to stick it to this "wild card." A surprisingly high number of jurors are swayed by emotion, led by who they like or dislike in rendering verdicts.

When an employee claims discrimination based on his or her inclusion in a protected category, the employer needs to negate the allegations with documentation to prove the company's action was based on something other than the worker's protected classification. When there is no documentation of the reasons for the termination because there was no reason, the ability to defend the assertions is virtually nonexistent.

If a company wants to fire someone because the wind was blowing from the south or because the employee wore purple shoes, it is legal, but they must be aware of the limited ability to defend successfully if sued. Consequently, while an employer can legally make an employment decision for absolutely no reason, it makes for very poor documentation when there is a claim of a wrongful termination. Good luck with a defense that is, "We did not fire him because of his National origin, we just canned him because . . . well, why the heck not." The jury will likely want to stick it to a callous boss.

That Is Just Mean

The scenario below is a good opportunity to evaluate the comprehension of the concept that discrimination is not illegal unless it is based on the person's inclusion in a protected category.

A woman applicant, Theresa Gee, is told she is a finalist for the receptionist position at corporate headquarters. She meets with the office manager, Jay Honeycutt, and the interview is proceeding in her eyes nicely.

Theresa tells Mr. Honeycutt, "I really hope I get this job. It is such a perfect fit."

Mr. Honeycutt looks at Theresa and says, "I am not sure how best to tell you this, but I have to be honest with you. Ms. Gee, you are the best person I have interviewed, but . . . I just can't give you this job. You are . . . just too ugly."

Theresa can't believe her ears. "I am not sure I understand."

"You are just at the back end of the attractive spectrum. I guess I would refer to your face as butt ugly or 'Bugly.' No offense intended. I just wanted to be upfront with you to help you. I would suggest you would be better off applying for positions that do not involve face time with . . . well, anyone who is not seeing impaired."

Theresa jumps up and says, "I am taking you to court."

Does Theresa have a good case? Mr. Honeycutt's actions are not only rude, but unfair right? The company is clearly discriminating based on a trait that has no bearing on how the potential candidate will perform the job. Further, any company that hires on looks is in big trouble, right?

Well . . . it is unfair and rude and downright mean, but is it actionable?

A plaintiff must prove by a preponderance of evidence that the employer has discriminated against them as a direct result of their inclusion in a protected category to be able to win their lawsuit for liability and damages. The specific protected categories are enumerated earlier in this chapter. Ugliness is not on that list. Consequently, the discrimination based on looks is not actionable unless the plaintiff can prove an element of discrimination based on one of the protected categories.

If, for example, the person could establish that their appearance could be considered a physical impairment and rises to level of a disability under the Americans with Disabilities Act (ADA) definition, they would have a claim. Or, if it could be proven that a company's definition of ugly encompasses characteristics that are associated with one of the other protected categories, including features distinctive to certain ethnicities, then that changes the case. If the plaintiff has no evidence to link the determination of ugliness to a protected category, the employer's refusal to hire the qualified, but ugly, Ms. Gee is legal.

As an aside, Mr. Honeycutt and any person performing the duties of interviewing and hiring should simply say, "Thank you for coming in. We so appreciate your time, and we will get back to you within two weeks with our decision."

There is rarely a need to outline reasoning for not hiring directly to the applicant. It is, however, imperative that the reasons for all hiring decisions be well documented to preserve evidence to defend a future claim of discrimination.

While it is presumed all employees are At-Will unless they have an employment contract, it is important that all companies make sure their employment documents from manuals to handbooks reiterate, without any wiggle room, that all employees are At-Will employees.

The following chapters in this section expand on each protected category and will help students and professionals build a better foundation for recognizing issues that arise when handling employee complaints utilizing the CIDER method. Knowledge is the key to teaching and training staff to make the company's environment a better place to work and to prevent improper behavior and illegal discrimination. Understanding the thrust of each classification is crucial to recognize the intricacies and potential pitfalls in evaluating employment complaints.

Sexual Harassment and Gender Discrimination

The placement of this protected category in the first spot, contrary to speculation, was not determined by throwing a dart at a board that listed the chapters. The Me-Too Movement combined with the escalation of employee complaints in the area of sexual harassment has made understanding and recognizing this imperative.

Companies need to encourage the reporting of inappropriate behavior. It takes courage for employees to report inappropriate conduct of a coworker because of stigma, peer pressure to ignore, and the fear that they will not be believed. When employees realize their unacceptable behavior will be reported and will not be tolerated by the employer, changes for the better as far as professionalism and a safer work environment will occur.

The days of a manager faced with a report of sexual conduct saying, "Rupert is a really good guy." Or, "Lester didn't mean anything, he's just a harmless flirt," or the classic, "boys will be boys" must be eliminated.

When employees know the workplace climate is to immediately report any behavior that makes others within the business feel uncomfortable, they will consider their words and actions more carefully.

Sexual harassment at its core involves treatment that is sexual in nature covering a wide range of acts that cause harm or discomfort. What is shocking to many people under 40 years of age is that prior to the mid-1970s, there was no such thing as a sexual harassment lawsuit. It did not exist.

In 1974 if a boss said to an employee, "Hey, honey, if you want to keep your job, you need to have sex with me," there were no options for that person except to say "No, thank you," and hope she would not be dismissed, or she could quit . . . or have sex with the boss.

A supervisor could fire an employee who would not sleep with him without any repercussions as long as he did not physically force himself on the person. Many a boss thought, "Hey, if she doesn't like my relentless come-ons, she can quit."

When a person at a bar asks another patron if they want to get out of there and go somewhere private, the parties are on equal footing. The person being asked feels no pressure or conflict. When a person in authority in an employment setting makes the same request, it is not between two equals because the supervisor has power over the other.

Fortunately, social norms and laws have changed, and now even the most clueless manager knows he cannot legally ask an employee for sexual favors as a trade-off for some job benefit.

The United States Supreme Court, in the case of Meritor Savings Bank v. Vinson, made it clear that a consensual sexual relationship with a boss does not equal a welcome relationship (Meritor Savings Bank v. Vinson, 477 U.S. 57 [1986]). The Court also said for the first time that sexual harassment, which creates a hostile or abusive work environment is a violation of Title VII of the Civil Rights Act of 1964.

The next major U. S. Supreme Court case that recognized the right of a person to bring a sexual harassment lawsuit was the landmark case of Harris v. Forklift Systems, which defined a discriminatorily abusive work environment with the term "hostile work environment," (Harris v. Forklift Systems Inc., 510 U.S. 17 [U.S. Supreme Ct. 1993]).

The Harris opinion held: when a workplace is permeated with intimidation, ridicule, and insult that alters the conditions of the victim's employment creating an abusive working environment, that constitutes discrimination. Further, the conduct need not "seriously affect (an employee's) psychological well-being" or lead the plaintiff to suffer injury. Prior to this case, a plaintiff had to show serious psychological damage to meet the burden of proving liability against the employer.

The two Supreme Court cases of Harris and Meritor changed the employment law landscape forever allowing employees to have a stronger legal basis for bringing sexual harassment lawsuits against their employers.

When looking at sexual harassment in the employment realm, it is important to understand the two main categories.

Quid Pro Quo

Quid Pro Quo is in play when one person has power over another employee. Quid Pro Quo roughly translated from Latin means "this for that" or in this context offering an employee some tangible employment benefit in exchange for something sexual.

For instance: An employee asks their boss for a raise, and the boss says, "If you want a raise, you need to sleep with me." This is classic Quid Pro Quo sexual harassment offering some job benefit in return for a sexual favor. This form of sexual harassment has really morphed into a supervisor's creation of a hostile working environment for a subordinate (a.k.a. supervisor sexual harassment) since it involves situations where someone has authority, real or perceived, over the other.

Even though there is no subtlety in this type of bold sexual harassment, it still exists. Most of the examples in this area of sexual harassment tend to be women being victimized by men. This may be perceived to be male bashing, but the EEOC states the vast majority of sexual harassment complaints are made by women against men (Charges Alleging Sexual Harassment FY 2010–FY 2018. Retrieved from https://www.eeoc.gov/eeoc/statistics/enforcement/sexual_harassment_new.cfm). Consequently, the male bashing is justified.

That does not mean women do not harass men, but there are other factors at play. Some men do not always fully appreciate the different perspectives of women. The point is that women and all employees just want to be able to go to work, do their jobs, and be respected without being subjected to harassment or inappropriate treatment simply based on their gender. This is another reason why educating all employees is so crucial to changing the culture. The importance of teaching and training workers in this area is discussed in greater detail later in the chapter.

Supervisor sexual harassment is held to a much higher standard than when there is no authority from the harasser over the victim. The supervisor's actions carry more weight because they can hire, fire, promote, and demote. A recent decision narrowed the definition of supervisor by saying that an employee is a "supervisor" for purposes of vicarious liability under Title VII only if he or she is empowered by the employer to take tangible employ-

© fizkes/Shutterstock.com

ment actions against the victim (Vance v. Ball State University, 570 U.S. 421 [2013]). Employers should assume this view may be modified by the courts to include reasonably perceived authority as well actual authority.

Consider this scenario. The names and job titles have been changed to protect the identity of the parties. Debbie and Terrell both work for Ajax Financial. Debbie has worked as Terrell's administrative assistant for over 4 years. Terrell is the Chief Financial Officer (CFO) for the company. He is Debbie's supervisor by all definitions. They are both single. Debbie decides that she wants to take this big leap of faith after deliberating the pros and cons for months.

She walks into Terrell's office, closes the door and begins, "I have been working up the courage to talk to you about this issue for months. We have been working so closely for over 4 years. I respect you as a person more than you could ever know. You are kind, smart, and considerate. We get along so well and our relationship has continued to grow and mature. We share our lives, and our time together has been life affirming.

"I know you would never ask me out on a date because you are too professional. But I would regret it the rest of my life if I did not try to give us a chance. I think you are special and know when we are together it is truly magical. I don't want to look back on this and see what we could have had when the opportunity for love is right in front of us.

"I want you to come over to my house for dinner. I will sign anything to make it clear I asked you out and you did not initiate this. I just don't want to have any regrets and know we are meant to be happy together."

So . . . is this okay if Terrell goes to Debbie's house in light of her willingness to execute a document that he did not ask her out, but she asked him out?

Ah . . . NO!

This is still a supervisor dating a person over whom they have authority. Only a few things can happen in the future. At some point either he will end the romantic relationship or she will end the romantic relationship. Then how will those yearly performance reviews and evaluations proceed? Supervisors should never date employees over whom they have power. This must be stressed continually in management meetings and reiterated in the company manual.

Some of the romantics in the audience may be saying, "What about the third option? Debbie and Terrell get married and live happily ever after!" An employer should not take those odds. Do not allow supervisors to date their underlings, because when it goes bad, the underling has a great sexual harassment case claiming they felt pressured to enter or remain in a relationship. In addition, even if neither of the parties involved in the affair complain, other employees may perceive favorable treatment is being given based on a sexual relationship and that may lead to other employee complaints.

Quid pro quo liability is absolute. The only defense the employer has is if the company can show that the employee suffered no tangible employment action stemming from the harassment. A tangible employment action is defined as "a significant change in employment status, such as hiring, firing, failing to promote, reassignment with significantly different responsibilities, or a decision causing a significant change in benefits" (Peoples v. The Marjack Company, Inc. et al., No. 8:2008cv00178—Document 70 [D. Md. 2010]).

But the courts have said that if the employee quits as a result of the sexual harassment, this alone may constitute a tangible employment action referred to as "constructive discharge." Consequently, if a person calls an employment attorney and says, "My supervisor just asked me to go out on a date to get the corner office," the lawyer may advise the employee to quit, thus taking away the employer's only viable defense to the quid pro quo harassment.

However, if an employee on the lowest rung of the company's hierarchy is working in the mail room and walks into the office of the vice-president of the company and says to her, "Hey, baby, if you want your mail delivered on time, you better deliver to me, if you know what I mean," and slaps her on the backside; this is not quid pro quo since the idiot who says this has no power over the woman. This vice-president is in control and can stop this by saying, "You are fired." While the low-level employee is not engaging in quid pro quo sexual harassment, this type of atmosphere, if allowed to exist, can create a hostile work environment.

Hostile Work Environment—Sexual Harassment

Quid pro quo is such an obvious form of sexual harassment that it is easier to train employees to recognize its existence. Co-employee sexual harassment, however, can be much subtler, creating a bigger challenge for human resource personnel to identify and prevent through teaching. Seminars in this area must address the problems directly. Any employee in the organization can create a hostile work environment through their actions and inappropriate comments.

Some employees will ask, "What can I do to avoid saying the wrong thing? I have trouble seeing the problem." Here is a simple answer: if you wouldn't say it or do it to one sex, then don't say it or do it to the other. That includes the tone and mannerisms that go along with the words.

Or offer another approach. Prior to uttering the questionable quip or joke, imagine if the same comment were said to someone important to them by one of their coworkers. Would they find it disgusting, offensive, or a come-on?

Some people will lament, "All this politically correct stuff is ruining all our fun." And they are right . . . it is ruining . . . their fun because they mistakenly think a working environment filled with sexual innuendo and overtly lewd comments is appropriate. But there are others who do not perceive it as fun and find it upsetting and deplorable.

This is not a case of majority rules. It does not matter if 95% of the employees are not bothered by the actions and behavior of some, the company must consider all employees.

For example, every time a woman smiles on a Monday morning, some meathead will say, "if you're smiling you must have gotten some action this weekend." There will be some who find it funny (hard to believe but there are those who still laugh when it is raining and someone says "nice weather . . . for ducks."), others who think it unprofessional but tolerate it, and there will be some who are made very uncomfortable by the remark. The company must not use majority rules mentality to ignore the behavior.

Sexual harassment takes many forms from innuendo, to a picture, to a gesture, and sometimes the lines are blurred. It is not sexual harassment for a man to see a woman in a new outfit and say, "You look very nice today." It is, however, not appropriate to say, "Whoa, you look so hot in that new outfit. It really shows your sexy body."

It is not always the words alone that convey a sexual component. If a person gets within 4 inches of his coworker and has Barry White music playing in the background and says, in a breathy soft whisper in her ear, "You look . . . really nice . . . today." The creepy alarm should be ringing off the hook.

Golden Rule

Remember learning the Golden Rule as a child? "Do unto others as you would have them do unto you."

It sounds nice, it sounds workable, it sounds like a can't miss concept, except for one thing—in the area of sexual harassment, following the golden rule can be a catastrophe.

What About Melvin

Melvin goes up to his coworker, Sheila. Neither of them are in a supervisory capacity nor has authority over the other. He looks at her and says,

"How are . . . you doing? Ya know, I could make you glad you're a woman. You know what I'm saying?

"I will make you scream your ABC's if ya know what I'm talking about.

"I could put the music in you, if you get my drift."

Now, this woman definitely gets his drift and should run, not walk but run, to her boss, or human resources, or to whomever to immediately report this behavior.

Sheila takes a moment to determine if she should simply tell Melvin he is a disgusting pig or file a complaint. She decides the best course of action would be to make his actions known to the employer. Her company, unfortunately, has not adopted the CIDER method. She seeks out her manager, Amy, who told her if she ever had a problem to contact her. Sheila outlines the specifics of Melvin's comments and questions.

Amy is in her second month on the job and, while nervous, knows she must bring Melvin into her office to go over the allegations. Amy has not been trained in the CIDER method. She is trying her best and begins, "Melvin, do you know Sheila in processing?'

"I sure do."

"Did you state to her you were going to make her glad she's a woman?"

"Absolutely," Melvin says grinning.

"You didn't actually tell her you would make her scream her ABC's, did you?"

"I sure did."

"Did you say that after you are done with her she will be singing, 'That's the way ah-ha ah-ha I like it?'"

"I gotta be honest with you, I don't remember saying that, but I really like that 'ah-ha, ah-ha I like it' line, and I am definitely adding that to my repertoire from now on."

A shell-shocked Amy continues, "Did you really say you would put the music in her?"

"Oh yeah."

And now this is where cluelessness and the golden rule collide.

Amy asks Melvin, "How would you feel if she said that stuff to you?!"

Melvin perks up and says, "Yeah baby! I would love it. That is why I said it to her, because I have been hoping she would say that stuff to me. I would love her to say that to me. The golden rule, baby. Do unto others as I want them to do to me."

Consequently, the golden rule needs to be modified for sexual harassment prevention. It should be, "do unto others as you would have them do unto you . . . if you actually understood their perspective."

The question often asked is, where is the line between boorish behavior and sexual harassment? Can an employee put their arm around a coworker? Can you say since they lost weight their body is smoking or that they smell fabulous? The law of sexual harassment is not about getting rid of workplace vulgarity nor does it outlaw sexually coarse and vulgar language that merely offends (Lyle v. Warner Brothers Television Production, 38 Cal. 4th 264 [2006]). The court in Lyle v. Warner Brothers reiterated that a harassing remark must be "objectively and subjectively offensive, one that a reasonable person would find hostile or abusive."

When evaluating the actions or words, the evaluator must determine if the behavior was respectful of the person's dignity. Taking this further, would a reasonable person interpret the conduct from the alleged perpetrator as unwelcome conduct of a sexual nature? If the behavior comes from a person of authority, it must be scrutinized much closer.

Training and Prevention

While not all men are as clueless as Melvin, there are degrees of obliviousness that cloud good judgment. If the employer assumes there is no need to educate because everyone in the organization understands the type of actions and comments that are inappropriate, they are ignoring the obvious. Without proper training and teaching all employees about unacceptable workplace behavior, employees will continue to pull a Melvin.

The current trend is that a company can reduce its liability if it has a well-defined sexual harassment policy in place which is taught and disseminated to all personnel.

There are wonderful model sexual harassment policies available from numerous sites. Employers should review and implement a formal policy as part of their company handbook to make sure that unwelcome sexual advances or questionable conduct which creates a hostile work environment are unequivocally denounced.

It is also imperative that all policies and training articulate that sexual harassment may also exist between same sex employees if the behavior is sexual in nature. Every employee should be aware through well-written policies, teaching, and preaching, that the company does not tolerate this type of conduct.

The adoption of well-articulated policies is just the beginning to properly prevent sexual harassment in the workplace. But while this is a good first step the company must go further.

Sexual harassment can be reduced by facing the common problems head on. Seminars and regular discussion to educate the staff will make a positive difference. Most people do not want to embarrass themselves or cause another person to have stress at work. Teaching employees what constitutes unacceptable behavior from all sides of the aisle will help the work environment. Group problem solving is an effective way to help employees see the issues from other perspectives to aid staff development. An environment of zero tolerance must be stressed continually, with all employees held accountable to the highest standard of behavior.

There are many good speakers and programs to flush out questionable conduct and help employees understand the underlying concepts. The burden of preventing sexual harassment is on the employer. Every company should strive with its actions to have a workplace that is free from harassment and discrimination. If employers fail to use due diligence in this area, they will be liable for damages.

Companies must not only train and teach, but must also make certain the lessons are learned. As discussed throughout this book, it is not enough to do the right thing; an employer must be able to prove they did the right thing. Consequently, some form of testing is necessary to document that the employees understand the information presented. Employees and students may attend seminars and meetings, but may be there in body only and be texting, daydreaming, or just not paying attention instead of learning. The testing forms will serve as written documentation of employee attendance and comprehension of the education process.

The anti-harassment training and teaching for all staff, as enumerated above, to remedy and prevent violations is imperative for every company. The goal is to make employees analyze their own behavior and understand how it can impact others. Fear is also a great motivator; training should include that the employee can be named personally in these harassment lawsuits and will be responsible to pay a monetary damage award to the victim (BC v. Steak N Shake Operations Inc., 512 S.W. 3d 276 [Texas Ct. of Appeals, 2017]).

Furthermore, the CIDER method should be implemented to make sure all complaints are handled properly. The employer must drive home the point that silence in regard to complaints is not the company's policy. Managers and supervisors must have additional training to monitor their employees to better recognize a sexually charged environment. An employer's claim that they were not aware of the sexual harassment is not a viable defense.

Unwelcome Behavior

Sexual harassment may be a picture put up on a bulletin board or a comment uttered in the office or a touch of a shoulder. It takes many forms, but once the employer is made aware of a concern, the manner of employer response will speak volumes as to the employee perception of the company's lack of tolerance.

© Pormezz/Shutterstock.com

The courts have said that to prevail on a claim of sexual harassment, a plaintiff must establish that: the person was subject to unwelcome sexual harassment, the conduct was severe or pervasive enough to cause a hostile work environment, and the conduct was directed at the person because of her or his sex (Clark County School District v. Breeden, 532 US 268, 121 [2001]).

There are four basic elements to understand in the sexual harassment arena. Was the behavior in question sexual in nature? Was the behavior one that a reasonable person in the victim's position would find inappropriate (objectively hostile)? Was the action unwelcome by the specific complainant? Was the conduct severe and pervasive enough to create an intimidating or hostile work atmosphere?

Victim's Point of View

Employers cannot make the error of focusing on their own opinion that most people in the complainant's position would not have a problem with the behavior of the alleged harasser.

The EEOC compliance manual indicates conduct should be judged from the viewpoint of the offended employee (Law & Guidance. n.d. Retrieved from https://www.eeoc.gov/policy/compliance.html). The reasonable person standard used in so many areas of the law should consider the victim's perspective.

Some forms of sexual harassment are so egregious that simply one incident by the offender is a no doubter, such as grabbing another employee's rear-end. Other behaviors such as jokes or flirting must be evaluated carefully to determine if they constitute sexual harassment. An employer will not be liable for every objectionable comment but will be found negligent if he or she was aware of the questionable behavior and allowed it to continue. The idea is not to make an employment setting sterile and without joy, but to recognize and weed out the behavior that is unwelcome.

Is asking a co-employee (with no supervisor status) to go out on a date sexual harassment? Not usually.

What about when the employee responds to the request for a date with, "No thank you," and the person asks them out a second time? Is that sexual harassment? Probably not, but starting to move toward crossing the line. The person again says, "No." Now the coworker comes back the third time and says, "Ok, I know you said no . . . twice, but I took a picture of you through your bedroom window plus using one of me in my underwear and photo-shopped them together to help you realize how great we would be as a couple. Now will you go out with me?" This behavior has clearly crossed the line and constitutes sexual harassment.

Once the victim makes the company aware that the action is unwelcome, the bar has been set. The company can no longer view the conduct complained of in a vacuum and speculate that the conduct is not so bad. The employer is now on notice that the behavior is unwelcome.

An employee suing an employer for sexual harassment was not an option prior to the mid-1970s, but now verbal and physical conduct of a sexual nature will give rise to employer liability.

When faced with an employee complaint, the company must determine if the conduct complained of explicitly or implicitly affects an individual's employment, unreasonably interferes with an individual's work performance, or creates an intimidating, or hostile work environment.

Instruction to employees to help them recognize sexual harassment combined with a system in place to encourage reporting of any inappropriate behavior is the best way to eliminate this form of discrimination in the workplace. But once a complaint is registered, the CIDER method must be implemented immediately.

Gender Discrimination

Gender discrimination occurs when an employee is treated unfavorably because of his or her sex. While it often manifests itself as sexual harassment that is not always the case. Judging women on how they look or dress while not applying the same standard to males in the workplace is gender discrimination. The laws of gender discrimination are there to protect both women and men. Hiring only women for certain positions, for example, as waitstaff, is gender discrimination toward men.

If one sex gets more time off than the other, this is likely gender discrimination. There must be a valid business reason beyond their sex for any benefit, including and especially salary. Gender discrimination also includes discrimination on the basis of childbirth and pregnancy. The Equal Pay Act of 1963 outlaws unequal pay on the basis of gender (Equal Pay Act of 1963 [Pub. L. 88-38] [EPA]).

If it can be proven that men are being paid more than women without any valid business reason, such as experience or sales results, that is illegal discrimination. Conversely if women are being paid more than men without an acceptable business reason, such as education or years of service, that is gender discriminatory. An employer may not use past women's salaries to justify paying women less than men for equal work (Rizo v. Yovino, No. 16-15372 J [9th Circuit Court of Appeals, 2018]).

If an employee is being passed over for a promotion because of sex, that is illegal discrimination. Years ago, women were not hired to be firefighters because . . . firefighting was classified as men's work. The logic to this practice was that women could not lift and carry as much as men. On average that is a correct statement, but applying a group average to one individual in the group is stereotyping. It is, however, acceptable to make sure a person can fulfill the essential duties of the job.

Fortunately, specific testing to prove the person is capable of performing the requirements of the job is the approved method to determine if a candidate meets the job qualifications instead of the old way of saying it is men's work.

No employer can treat a person unfavorably because of his or her sex. If a woman returns from having a baby and the employer changes her pay or does more than slightly modify her position, it may be gender discriminatory.

In the U.S. Supreme Court case of International Union, United Automobile Workers v. Johnson Controls, the employer barred women of childbearing age from certain jobs due to potential harm that could occur to a fetus (United Automobile Workers v. Johnson Controls, Inc. 499 U.S. 187 [1991]). The Court ruled that the employer's restriction against fertile women performing "dangerous jobs" constituted gender discrimination under Title VII. The fact that the job posed a risk to fertile women did not justify barring all fertile women from the position.

National Origin Discrimination

National origin discrimination in the workplace means an employer cannot allow harassment or make decisions based on culture, language, or dress associated with any national origin (country of origin).

The EEOC has stated that illegal discrimination in this area involves treating employees and applicants differently because they are from a certain country, because of ethnicity (including their accent), or because they appear to be of a certain ethnic background. In addition, national origin discrimination may involve disparate treatment because they are married to or associated with a person of a certain national origin.

The law forbids discrimination based on national origin for any aspect of employment, including hiring, firing, pay, job assignments, promotions, layoff, training, and fringe benefits.

Bona Fide Occupational Qualification

A major area of litigation within this protected category involves communication difficulties stemming from foreign accents. An employer may not base an employment decision on an employee's foreign accent unless it seriously interferes with the employee's job performance.

Bona fide occupational qualifications (BFOQ) are requirements that employers are allowed to consider in making employment decisions, but the qualification(s) must be essential to the success of the business. BFOQ is an exception and a valid defense for discrimination if it can be shown that the person cannot perform the essential duties of the position. The courts, however, scrutinize this defense narrowly because it is often used as an excuse for unnecessary discrimination against someone based on inclusion in a protected class. Chapters Eleven and Fourteen will discuss the BFOQ defense in greater depth with regard to religion and disability respectively.

If a person is a dispatcher, their accent may interfere with communication and thus would potentially qualify as a BFOQ defense to discrimination. The employer must prove that the communication concern is a disruption to the business. As with all defenses using BFOQ, the company must meet the burden to show that the issue in question affects the essential duties of the position and is not ancillary or minimal.

In the case of Arzate v. City of Topeka, the Hispanic plaintiff claimed the defendant's failure to promote him after 19 years as an animal control officer was based on his ethnicity (Arzate v. City of Topeka, 884 F. Supp. 1494 [D. Kan. 1995]). The defendant's defense was that the plaintiff's accent made it difficult to communicate the animal control policies to the public, and he could not understand written instructions from his supervisor. The court in this case found for the employer concluding that the employer's reasons were not based on discrimination but on reasonable business necessity (a valid BFOQ defense).

Proving the Case

To prove national origin discrimination, an employee or applicant must show they were subjected to a negative job action because of ethnicity, birthplace, ancestry, culture, native language, surname, accent, or other characteristics that are closely related to their country of origin.

It is quite rare that an employee will be able to present obvious proof of national origin discrimination such as a recording of several witnesses who will testify they heard the supervisor state, "I just don't like having Vietnamese people in accounting," or, "I will not ever make the mistake of hiring a Swedish person for a creative position again." Clear evidence like this would be termed a "smoking gun" or unequivocal proof of discrimination based on a protected category. In essence, a no-doubt-about-it piece of evidence that employment decisions are being made on the basis of national origin.

Proof is rarely as concrete as described in the preceding paragraph. The majority of trials on the issue of employer discrimination based on inclusion in a protected category are proven by circumstantial evidence allowing the fact finder to infer that discrimination was part of the decision-making process.

A plaintiff in these cases might present corroborating proof using past and present employee testimony to demonstrate a pattern exists of negative employment decisions based on an employee's inclusion in a protected class.

Case in point: an employee has been working for the company for 5 years with great evaluations. The supervisor learns that the employee is Iranian and fires him 4 weeks later. The employer will claim that the termination had nothing to do with his national origin. The trial will feature the presentation of evidence from prior and current employees as to past slights and issues regarding the protected category as well as testimony from the employee in question as to the problems encountered. The employer will defend by presenting evidence that the employment action was based on factors other than the employee's country of origin.

Companies must make sure they do not allow an environment where discrimination will go unchecked. Furthermore, the business must be able to offer concrete proof that all reported issues were acted upon using the CIDER method. The education must start at the top and be passed on to all staff in meetings, reviews, and seminars to ensure no decisions are ever made based on culture, language, or dress associated with that national origin.

Religion

The basic concept of this category is pretty straightforward. An employer cannot make an employment decision based on someone's religion or genuine religious beliefs. A hospital may not have a hiring policy that says we only hire or vastly prefer Jewish doctors. Conversely, a company may not say we are not hiring Muslims, or we will only promote Christians to management positions.

It is illegal to impose certain conditions of employment based on religion, with some exceptions such as a Rabbi needing to be Jewish or a Priest, Catholic (BFOQ), but unless there is a justifiable legally accepted reason, an employer cannot discriminate based on this category.

Religious Accommodation

In addition, there is another element to this category. An employer must make reasonable accommodations to the religious needs of employees where such need can be met without undue hardship on the conduct of the employer's business (Trans World Airlines Inc. v. Hardison, 432 U.S. 63 [1977]). The litigation in this area has increased significantly.

Prudent employers will err on the side of providing the religious accommodation when there is little hardship on the business such as allowing an employee regular breaks to pray four times per day or not work on a Sunday.

The employer has a right to determine that the religious belief is genuine. The EEOC defines religious practice to include moral or ethical beliefs as to what is right and wrong, which are sincerely held with the strength of traditional religious views.

As with all protected categories, employers need to understand their rights as well as employee rights to avoid liability for discrimination. A common problem is knowing when to challenge the issue and when to accommodate.

At one company, a new employee, Eleanor, says she cannot work on Sunday because of her religious beliefs, and the employer obliges her request. After 4 weeks, when three other employees realize the special treatment Eleanor receives come forward and say, "Hey, I am deeply religious too, so I can't work on Sunday." Now what happens?

The company doubts the sincerity of the three who seem to have suddenly found religion. What is the protocol? How does the company challenge the request without appearing unnecessarily adversarial?

If the matter proceeded to trial on the issue of the company failing to accommodate the religious request, an employer can present evidence that the challenger's beliefs are not sincere. But the employer needs to decide if the cost of defending a lawsuit is worth contesting the sincerity of the belief or the reasonableness of the accommodation. It is often a solid business decision in not allowing the matter to reach the level of a bitter dispute that will leave each party upset and unsatisfied.

If this were a disability case, the employer would simply request a doctor's report outlining the employee's limitations, which would help the company understand the necessary adaptations to meet the needs of the worker. But determining the sincerity of a religious belief is a more complicated issue. Requesting an employee's clergy to vouch for an employee's religious sincerity is an option but would not likely lead to concrete information. The employer must avoid the appearance of favoring certain religions by routinely questioning requests from employees of some faiths while consistently accepting accommodation from others. Whatever decision is reached must be documented.

An employer must be made aware of a belief or religious practice that is in conflict with the job duties before a duty to accommodate arises. However, the onus is on the company to prove it advised all staff of their rights to come forward with concerns, and a company must be able to prove the workers were informed of the rights to make the company aware of their needs in this area.

As with disability, an employer may defend their actions in not accommodating the religious based request by claiming undue hardship to the business.

BFOQ?

Minoj, a Hindu, has been working at a large grocery store for over 3 months. A truck pulls up to the loading dock and the manager asks him and two others to help unload the inventory.

Minoj goes out with the other two employees and realizes the job is to unload sides of beef into the large refrigeration storage locker in the butcher shop. He goes back inside and tells the manager that as a result of his religious beliefs, he is unable to unload this truck. He

© FoodAndPhoto/Shutterstock.com

is Hindu and considers the cow to be a sacred symbol of life that should be protected and revered.

The manager says, "This is a requirement of your job. If you are not going to help us out, you are not a team player and should find another job."

The manager has not been properly educated on accommodation and undue hardship. Minoj has worked at the store for over 3 months. Unloading beef is clearly not an essential duty of the job as this is the first time his presence was requested for that duty.

If, for example, Minoj was applying to work as a butcher's assistant, then the handling of beef would be an essential job duty. If the employer can prove that the job requires someone who is willing and able to handle meat regularly, this would be a BFOQ. But in the present case, unloading the sides of beef is a limited task, and the company could easily accommodate his religious beliefs.

The law in this area not only forbids religious discrimination, but makes harassment of employees on the basis of religion illegal. Consequently, employers must be cognizant of providing a workplace environment of equal treatment and free from ridicule.

A company must accommodate employee's beliefs and practices unless doing so would cause more than just minimal burden on the operation of the employer's business, according to the EEOC. Undue hardship is a viable defense, which considers cost, safety, efficiency, or the burden on other employees.

The most common accommodations are time off for observances, religious dress (such as Muslim head-dress), and flexible scheduling. The employer has a right to ask for more information to evaluate any request but must be wary of implicit discrimination based on using different standards. All decisions must be documented and placed in the appropriate files. The employer must also make sure it is providing equal and consistent accommodations to all employees, regardless of faith.

Nontraditional Religions

A problem arises when personal religious beliefs are not mainstream or accepted by traditional organized religions. In the 1997 case of Van Koten v. Family Health Management Inc., the plaintiff claimed he observed the religion of Wicca that carries with it the belief in astrology, psychic abilities, and that Halloween is a holy day (Van Koten v. Family Health Management, Inc., 955 F. Supp. 898 [N.D. Ill. 1997]). The employer said he would allow him to take Halloween off from work for religious observance. The court said it does not matter that Wicca is not organized or accepted by more than a few as long as they are sincerely held beliefs.

It is important to note that atheism is a religion for the purposes of protected category status. This legal classification is relevant because it means an employer cannot legally discriminate against an employee based on their atheism.

Holidays can bring on feelings of discrimination among minority religions. Is it religious discrimination to have Christmas music playing and the office decorated for the holidays?

Employers need to be sensitive to this aspect of religious discrimination. The majority rules mentality is generally a poor method for handling any employment issue.

An atheist who sees company sponsored Christmas décor all around them may bypass the complaint procedure, quit, and bring a hostile work environment lawsuit because they would argue the company not only had knowledge of the situation, but promoted holiday décor with company sponsored actions. Employees may perceive their supervisor's religious expression as coercive, even if it is not intended as such. Consequently, supervisors must be cognizant of not appearing to use their authority to either require or discourage religious expression among their employees as a condition of employment.

It is crucial that businesses promote and embrace religious diversity. Every business must consult a calendar listing every holiday from all religions to avoid scheduling a training session on Yom Kippur, a company picnic during Ramadan, or the company party on Christmas Eve.

A case that emphasizes the crux of the concept is Peterson v. Wilmur Communications, Inc. (Peterson v. Wilmur Communications, Inc., 205 F. Supp. 2d 1014 [E.D. Wis. 2002]). In that case, the court held that White Supremacy can be classified as a religion. The employee in question claimed he had a belief system that was termed Creativity. The belief system of the employees claimed religion had, at its core, disgusting, abhorrent ideas that should be insulting to all people. Their teachings describe a Utopian white supremacist world and mandates that such a world can only be established through denigration of nonwhites.

The employer in this case became aware of the plaintiff's religious beliefs when a story appeared in a local paper. As a result of seeing the story, the employer demoted the plaintiff to a position with no supervisory duties since neither he nor any employee could be sure of his objectivity because of his racist beliefs.

His employer claimed that Creativity was not a religion. The employer said that even if the court found that it was a religion, there was justifiable business reason (BFOQ) for the demotion. The court disagreed. Here was the problem: the employer made his employment decision solely based on the worker's religious beliefs instead of waiting for some inappropriate action or decision to justify the negative employment action. If the company had demoted him for treating an employee unjustly, they would be on strong legal ground; but instead the employer only responded to the religious convictions. The decision to punish the employee was made solely as a result of the employee's stated religious beliefs, and that was found to be religious discrimination.

The employer must also make sure there is no harassment occurring on the basis of religion. Harassment must be more than rude or insensitive to be actionable. It must rise to a level of being so pervasive that it unreasonably interferes with work performance. The company should not wait until the problem builds but must immediately address and correct any inappropriate comments as soon as the business is aware of the situation (EEOC v. Sunbelt Rentals 521 F.3d 306 [4th Cir. 2008]).

Race and Color

Even though this chapter features both race and color, they are not synonymous.

It is illegal for employers to discriminate on the basis of an unchangeable characteristic associated with race, such as skin color, hair texture, or certain facial features even though not all members of the race share the same characteristic. The law also prohibits discrimination on the basis of a condition that predominantly affects one race.

Color discrimination can occur between persons of different races or ethnicities, or between persons of the same race or ethnicity. The language of the Title VII Act of 1964 does not define color, but various court decisions have defined color as pigmentation, complexion, skin shade, or tone. Color discrimination occurs when treatment is based on someone's lightness, darkness, or other color characteristic.

When evidence is presented in a courtroom of a company systematically getting rid of dark-skinned black employees and hiring light skinned blacks, it is not a viable defense for an employer to say, "Well, while we did fire an African-American, we did hire an African-American to fill her spot, so clearly no discrimination." This would be discrimination based on color.

In enforcing Title VII's prohibition of race and color discrimination, the EEOC has adjudicated a large number of cases since 1964. Under the E-RACE Initiative, the Commission continues to be focused on the eradication of race and color discrimination and address contemporary forms of overt, subtle, and implicit bias. It is enlightening and instructive to review the many case summaries on their website outlining numerous instances of discrimination based on race and color. The EEOC site, Eradicating Racism and Colorism from Employment is at https://www.eeoc.gov/eeoc/initiatives/e-race/caselist.cfm and well worth reviewing in depth.

An employer also violates the law where it can be shown that the company is isolating certain employees based on their race or color from other employees or from customer contact or assigning staff to predominantly minority establishments or geographic areas based on color or race.

It is illegal for a company to make racially motivated decisions; race or color can never be a BFOQ. An employer may not legally determine that they will place certain races or certain people of color in certain locations because they think it will be better for business.

Applications and resumes cannot be labeled in any manner to designate an applicant's race or color. Furthermore, any attempt to access information that tends to disclose an applicant's race will be found to imply that that race or color was utilized as a factor in the company's ultimate hiring decisions.

Age

Age was added as a protected class under the ADEA (Age Discrimination Employment Act) in 1967. Consider these two examples.

A candidate for the job of radio disc jockey comes to the station for the interview. Kendra is 30 years old and applying for the job of 2:00–6:00 pm weekday drive time shift at KBLA. This station plays oldies, not from the 70s and 80s, but real oldies from the World War II era, the Big Band sounds like Benny Goodman ("Who is he?" virtually everybody reading this thinks to themselves). The station bills themselves as "Swing Radio—dedicated to keeping the Big Band sounds alive and well."

Kendra has worked as a disc jockey for 13 years and has excellent references. The station manager meets with her and at the conclusion of the interview says, "Kendra, I just can't give you this job. You don't understand the big band sounds. You don't know what was going on in our country during the 40s and 50s, the sacrifice and the lack of divisiveness. In reality, you are just too young for this job."

Kendra dejectedly leaves the station and wonders if this is a great case for age discrimination.

The second example also concerns a candidate for a job as an on-air radio personality. The job opening is at the FM radio powerhouse WNOW as a disc jockey. This candidate, Isaac, is 48 years of age. He has been working in the field for over 13 years. WNOW's slogan is, "We play today's best music and only the hottest songs."

Isaac meets with the program director who also handles the hiring of all on-air personalities. Isaac reiterates his vast experience in the field. The program director puts his hand up to stop Isaac from talking and says, "Isaac, I just can't hire you. You are not really the type of person we are looking for. I mean you probably believe Flo Rida is a state and think 50 Cent is a coin and not Curtis James Jackson III. You are just too old for the job."

Isaac leaves and wonders if he has a viable age discrimination case.

In both these examples there is clearly age discrimination. Neither was tested to determine if they were knowledgeable in regard to the areas of concern to the hiring directors. The decision to not hire them was based on their age, not on their actual knowledge gleaned from a valid testing method.

While both examples are age discrimination, only one of the candidates has a good employment law case. The reason is, the protected category is age 40 and over. It is not the entire spectrum of all ages. Why? Because 30-year-old employees do not need protection. Congress realized that the problem was with older employees. Consequently, the protection for age discrimination in employment only extends to individuals who are 40 years old and greater.

Many employers were systematically getting rid of older workers because they cost the company more than younger staff members. The medical benefits provided for workers are significantly more expensive for older employees based on insurance rates that are calculated using age as one relevant factor to determine premiums.

Furthermore, individuals employed with a company for 25 years have attained a salary much higher than the starting wage of an employee with far less experience. Consequently, a company could save a great deal of money by terminating senior staffers and hiring younger ones. Congress, seeing this serious problem, enacted the ADEA to combat this trend.

An interesting problem crops up with this category. Many job applications have a question asking, "What year did you graduate from high school?" This is an illegal question. It is not that an FBI agent is going to burst through the door and say, "Ok, whoever wrote that question is under arrest. Cuff him."

As with many improper questions the problem only comes to light if it is challenged.

Harold applies for a job with Acme Furniture Movers. He answers the question that he graduated from Duluth Central High School in 1988. Acme does not hire Harold. Harold retains an employment law attorney and sues Acme Furniture Movers for age discrimination.

The trial begins and the human resource director for Acme is on the witness stand. Harold's lawyer begins her cross-examination.

"Why did your company want to know the year Harold graduated from high school?"

"I didn't even realize we asked that question."

"Well, I am directing you to your own job application form. Do you agree that line 14 asks the date and year an applicant graduated from high school?

"Yeah, it definitely asks that."

"You will note Harold answered that he graduated high school in 1988. How old would you estimate Harold is from that answer?"

"Well people are usually 18 years of age when they graduate, and that was like 30 years ago, so about 48 years old."

"That is correct. I ask you, what reason would your company ask an applicant the year of their high school graduation except to know how old he is?"

"Ok, I know there must be a good reason if it is on our preprinted application, so it is because, I guess I am not sure . . ."

The buzzer has just sounded. "Thank you for playing. Do we have some parting gifts for this company that is about to lose this age discrimination case?"

The company is in real trouble because there are very few valid reasons to inquire about an applicant's high school graduation date except to see how old he or she is. If there is no reason to ask a question except to learn about an applicant's inclusion in a protected category, do not ask it. This recommendation is covered in more depth in Chapter Sixteen on Hiring Issues.

The ADEA protects workers age 40 and over from discrimination in all employment practices, including harassment. It can be difficult for employers to differentiate between harmless kidding and harassment. Should employers put a stop to the behavior when employees call an older employee, "grandpa" or put a walker by his chair?

The key question that must be asked is if the conduct is unwelcome in the victim's perspective. Simple teasing, offhand comments, and isolated incidents will not amount to actionable discrimination unless a plaintiff can prove the conduct is unwelcome, unreasonably affects performance, and is pervasive.

Once an employee registers a complaint, the CIDER method will flush out the details for an employer to properly evaluate if the kidding rises to the level of harassment. The appropriate response will be based on the ultimate determination.

A highly litigated area of employment law is disability discrimination. Disability is a protected category stemming from the ADA enacted in 1990 emphasizing that it is illegal to discriminate against a disabled individual in the workplace. The thrust of these laws is to recognize that discrimination impedes those with disabilities from obtaining jobs that they are qualified to perform and to eliminate that bias (The Americans with Disabilities Act of 1990 [42 U.S.C. § 12101]).

There is a difference in the disability category versus other protected categories. A person with an ADA disability may have limitations that hinder his or her abilities on the job as opposed to the other protected categories where there is rarely any limitation that makes performing the job an issue.

Defined

Just because a person cannot perform his or her job due to physical or emotional limitations, that does not mean he or she is disabled as defined by the ADA. The ADA definition of disability is really less medical oriented and more legal, stating that: "Disability is a physical or mental impairment that substantially limits one or more major life activities."

The ADA definition of disability is the criteria for determining if a person is in the protected class based on disability.

Take this example: Ashley is a construction worker. An injury prevents her from lifting more than 50 lb and she cannot return to her construction position. Although she is disabled from her occupation, she may not meet the definition of disability pursuant to the ADA. In Toyota Motor Manufacturing v. Williams, the high court ruled that under the ADA, the inability to perform occupation-specific tasks does not necessarily mean that the employee is substantially limited in performing a major life activity (Toyota Motor Manufacturing v. Williams, 534 U.S. 184, 122 S. Ct. 681 [2002]).

The terms "substantially limited" and "major life activities," the key phrases in the ADA definition of disability, are subject to interpretation and oftentimes are the focus of the legal dispute in regard to disability cases. Major life activity is presently defined as tasks of central importance to people's lives.

The court cases often center on the plaintiff's ability to care for oneself from bathing to hygiene. There are more than a few cases determining if a person is disabled under the ADA that devote an inordinate amount of the opinion to analyzing the plaintiff's time and difficulties to brush their teeth, shampoo their hair, and get dressed.

The phrase, "substantially limited" is periodically interchanged with "severely limited." The impairment does not have to be permanent to be substantially limited. Substantially limited has been defined as "significantly restricted as to the condition, manner or duration under which an individual can perform a particular major life activity as compared to the condition, manner, or duration under which the average person in the general population can perform that same major life activity" (Verdi v. Potter, 2010 U.S. Dist. LEXIS 11053 [E.D.N.Y. Feb. 9, 2010]).

An individual is not disabled nor in the protected class under the ADA definition simply because his or her physician states that the person is disabled. A doctor's report stating that the employee is disabled is not necessarily an analysis of the patient's condition compared to the very specific ADA criteria the court found in Toyota Motor Manufacturing v. Williams.

Clayton is a major league pitcher who throws 95 mph. He suffers a rotator cuff injury and he cannot throw more than 75 mph. His pitching career is over. He is disabled from his job, yet his physical impairment does not substantially limit him in major life activities because those are defined tasks of central importance to a person's life. And while baseball and his career are important, the courts focus on taking care of himself from showering to getting dressed as major life activities, and Clayton is able to do virtually anything except get major league hitters out. Consequently, Clayton is not disabled under the ADA despite being disabled from his job.

Work restrictions that transfer into daily life are sometimes classified as major life activities; keyboarding is one example.

Is a worker disabled and thus in a protected class if he or she is totally hearing impaired in one ear? What if he lost his pinky finger; is a diabetic; has a 15% impairment to her lower back? Each case must be analyzed individually and sometimes very similar impairments will result in different findings in regard to disability.

The ability to lift a particular weight shows inconsistency in these cases. A lifting impairment without evidence of other restrictions is generally insufficient to meet the definition of disability. The person must prove that the restriction substantially limits major life activities. There are cases that have found that a lifting restriction of 15 lb is substantially limiting (Lowe v. Angelo's Italian Foods, 87 F.3d 1170 [10th Cir. 1996]), while other cases with even higher weight limits have been determined not to meet the ADA criteria of a disability.

Mental Disability

Mental impairment is a very difficult issue because of the problems with classifying and identifying mental impairments. Imagine a pilot who suffers from depression as a disability and claims the inability to concentrate. How does an employer accommodate that? Is it a business necessity or a BFOQ that pilots have no mental issues?

The courts generally have been unsympathetic to opining that depression is a disability, but more open to classifying a bipolar diagnosis as meeting the ADA definition of disability. As with all claimed disabilities and requests for accommodation, the employer has an absolute right to request proof by a physician.

There will be times when all the available facts will not reveal a clear picture confirming or denying the status. The company must analyze the restrictions in light of the ADA definition and document the process and reasoning for the ultimate determination.

Employers Are Never Forced to Hire Unqualified Workers

There are some who voice the complaint, "All these laws are forcing companies to hire unqualified individuals for jobs." That is not true and fosters misguided application of the law.

Consider the example of Joel and the trucking company.

Joel worked as a truck driver for 10 years for Acme Trucking until he suffered a boating accident. As a result of the serious injuries from that incident, he is now totally blind. After recovering from his injuries (although the blindness is permanent), Joel applies for a bus driving position with a new company, Speedy Trucking, and makes no mention of his loss of sight.

The manager of Speedy Trucking talks to Joel at length over the telephone and informs him that they were very impressed with his resume. The manager specifically says, "Joel, I gotta tell you, based on this phone interview, your past driving experience and letters of reference from your prior job at Acme Trucking, you are perfect for our job opening of over the road truck driver."

The manager of the trucking company concludes the telephone interview by saying, "Come in tomorrow. We will finalize the paperwork and get you started driving right away."

Joel excitedly says, "Great, I will be in at 9:00 am sharp."

At exactly 9:00 am the next day Joel is escorted in to the manager's office accompanied by his service dog.

Joel reaches his hand out and says to the manager, "I can't wait to get back to driving."

The manager looks at him and says, "Are you blind?"

Joel sits down and explains, "Yes, I lost my sight a year ago in a boating accident. I can't wait to see my truck and get on the route."

"But you can't see."

"Oh, I see the irony. Yeah, that is a bit of drawback, but I have a GPS on my phone so I'll be fine."

The manager says, "I can't hire a blind person to drive a truck."

© Andrey Tirakhov/Shutterstock.com

"Wait a minute, you were going to hire me, but then you discovered I am totally blind and now you won't hire me?"

"Right."

"You understand total blindness is a disability under the ADA definition, right?"

"Yes, but . . ."

"And you understand disability is a protected category, right?"

"Yes."

"So, you are admitting the only reason you are not hiring me is based on my inclusion in a protected category."

"I am telling you I am not hiring a blind truck driver."

Joel stands up and exclaims, "I am suing for illegal discrimination."

As set forth earlier, while anybody can sue for anything, Joel's case against Speedy Trucking is not a viable lawsuit. Nothing in the law compels a company to hire or retain a person who cannot perform the obligations and responsibilities of the job. As discussed previously in Chapters Ten and Eleven, the defense of BFOQ allows a limited exception for discrimination if it can be demonstrated that the person cannot perform the essential duties of the position. The point is no employer is ever compelled to hire an unqualified person for a job.

The BFOQ defense allows a business to discriminate legally against a person with no legs who is applying for the job of lifeguard at the beach. BFOQ may also be used as a defense to a claim of gender discrimination when a restaurant will not consider males for the women's bathroom attendant position.

In determining whether illegal discrimination has occurred under the ADA, it is irrelevant that the employer did not intend to discriminate. But discriminatory actions are permissible if they are job related and necessary for the business and if the required job performance cannot be accomplished with reasonable accommodation. Hence, Speedy Trucking Company will be able to successfully use the defense of BFOQ to discriminate against Joel, the blind applicant for the driving job, based on his inclusion in the protected category.

Accommodation for Disabled Employees

It is not only illegal to discriminate against a disabled worker, but in addition, the employer has a proactive obligation to make reasonable accommodations to the known physical and mental limitations of an otherwise qualified individual with a disability (Lyons v. Legal Aid Society, 68 F.3d 1512 [2d Cir.1995]). Accessibility is not just a good idea; it is the law pursuant to the ADA.

Reasonable accommodation would include making all employee areas accessible, modifying equipment such as computers and desks, and providing interpreters for blind or deaf workers.

Certain accommodations, such as an entrance ramp or wider bathroom stalls are well understood, but the issues can become more complicated when determining the appropriate methods for making a reasonable accommodation. How far must an employer go? Wouldn't it be easier and oftentimes less expensive just to hire a nondisabled worker?

Yes, sometimes it is easier, and that is why the laws were enacted—to protect a group of people in which societal norms and beliefs make it a desirable goal to eliminate bias.

The potential modifications and adjustments to the work environment must be considered and evaluated on a case-by-case basis to determine what is reasonable. In considering the proper accommodations, a company must carefully review the essential functions of the job and compare them with the specific limitations of the disabled worker.

An employer may need and can request additional information to evaluate the situation from health care professionals. A company has a right to confirm that the person claiming disability is actually disabled and be informed of his or her specific limitations.

The ADA does not require an employer to reasonably accommodate an employee who does not make his or her disability known to the employer unless it is obvious. The employer may legally require documented proof of a disability before accommodating the worker. An employer should not start accommodating an employee based on limited information. The best time to obtain detailed information is at the onset of the claim, not 2 years later.

Requesting a doctor's opinion for analyzing employee accommodations should be handled carefully and thoughtfully to avoid an adversarial implication. Soliciting an opinion from a professional who is not the employee's treating physician may give the appearance of an attempt to dispute the accommodation instead of a request for assistance to make the best possible decision. However, that may be a necessary step if the company believes the employee's doctor is being more of an advocate than trying to educate.

The company need not simply follow the request of the disabled worker to alter the working conditions. Reasonable accommodation does not necessarily mean total accommodation. The employer has a right to decide the final accommodation to offer the employee after considering all aspects. A company should explore and document all viable alternatives, and when the decision is reached as to the accommodations, that proposal should be made in writing to document the offer. Further, all responses and agreements from the employee in question regarding the proposed accommodation must be documented.

Undue Hardship

Is there anything the employer can claim to justify not accommodating the disabled employee? The ADA lists several ways for the employer to defend a decision not to accommodate:

- Undue hardship creating significant difficulty or expense;
- Stress on other workers;
- Danger to self or others.

The defense of undue hardship is a determination based on many factors including the size and profits of the company and many other factors versus the cost and disruption to the business. As with all aspects of the employment area, the considerations, cost analysis, and all other factors researched in depth must be documented to meet any allegations of failure to accommodate.

Increasingly, disabled employees request to work at home instead of coming to an office. There is no requirement that an employer must honor this offer, but this, as with any requested accommodation, must be thoroughly analyzed to determine if it is a viable alternative. The limitations of the disabled employee compared with the essential duties of the job functions must be scrutinized and documented.

Some jobs lend themselves to the work-at-home option. If it turns out marginal duties can be assigned to someone else in the office, and the crux of the disabled employee's job can be virtually as effective at home, then working out of the home may be a reasonable accommodation to the disabled worker. There are some jobs, however, where the work at home option is not practical. If a waiter at the restaurant says he or she needs to work out of the home, that request would be a no-brainer to refuse based on undue hardship. Each request must be evaluated comparing reasonableness to the essential duties of the position.

An accommodation that fundamentally alters the business is also not reasonable. For example, a Laser Tag facility would not be forced to provide bright lighting for a visually impaired employee because that proposed accommodation would drastically alter the business. Whether an accommodation is reasonable under the ADA is determined by considering all relevant factors including hardship and cost to the employer.

This area can be fraught with difficulties since some impairments are complex to dissect and handle. The case of Davis v. Utah State Tax Commission concerned an employee who had multiple chemical sensitivities (MCS) and requested a move away from a coworker who wore extremely strong perfume (Davis v. Utah State Tax Commission, 96 F. Supp. 2d 1271 [D. Utah 2000]). The difficulty of the situation for employers is heightened when the disability is not apparent, and the medical science is not clear or universally accepted.

The plaintiff had originally requested to work out of her home, but the employer refused stating that as a worker for the state tax office handling confidential information, working at home was not a viable alternative.

The employer determined the best accommodation was to move Davis (the plaintiff), but then the new position brought her close to a person whose hand lotion aggravated her symptoms. The employer could not get an agreement from the coworker to stop wearing hand lotion.

The scent-averse employee quit and sued the employer for failing to accommodate. The company did not have well-documented evidence that they had carefully considered the various possibilities for accommodating the employee in relation to the claimed medical condition.

The lesson learned from this decision is that the employer must document that they went through the interactive process to evaluate all reasonable accommodations as well as being open to adopting a simple accommodation (the employee had suggested moving to an area with other employees who were not wearing skin applicants) when it is not a significant hardship.

The CIDER Method and Accommodation

The CIDER method should also be utilized whenever accommodation is requested by an employee. It is imperative that all evaluations and determinations of accommodations be handled in a systematic manner to document all the factors and options considered to prove either undue hardship or that the company's choice for accommodation is reasonable.

The point is that employers must be aware of their need to document and justify their decisions to prove good faith efforts. A reasonable accommodation must be an effective accommodation. It does not need to be perfect nor does it need to be what the employee requested as long as accommodation is effective and meets the criteria to ensure equal opportunity in the employment process.

Not an Exhaustive List

There is no complete list of every disability that an employee may have. The ADA definition is the key to assess if a particular employee is disabled. Some conditions rise to the level of meeting the criteria only at the more severe end of the condition such as Asthma or Tourette Syndrome. Alcoholism and drug addiction have been found to be disabilities, leading to some confusion.

Otis is caught drinking on the job. Just as the boss is about to say, "Pack up your stuff and leave, you're fired," Otis says, "Oh, sorry for guzzling a pint of tequila at my desk, but I am an alcoholic, so I am in a protected class cuz I am disabled."

The law in this area is designed not to protect Otis, but to protect Ralph. Ralph has worked for the company for 5 years. One day he walks in to his manager's office and says "This is a big day for me. It is the fifteenth anniversary of my sobriety."

"Oh, you had a problem?"

"Yeah, I had to go through in-patient treatment to help me fight my alcoholism, but I have not had a drink in fifteen great years."

"Ralph, fifteen years sober, that is really, really fantastic! Oh, and you are fired."

An employer cannot do that without legal ramifications.

Drug addiction and alcoholism are only protected disabilities in that a person cannot be fired or demoted because of the stigma of the condition. That is far different from being fired for using or drinking on the job. Otis can be fired for drinking on the job even though he is an alcoholic. Ralph cannot be fired for the stigma of his condition.

What is crucial to understand, however, is that an employer cannot treat workers differently based on their inclusion in a protected class. Consequently, if a company gives women a reprimand when they are intoxicated on the job but fires men who are intoxicated, that is discrimination based on protected status (gender). If a business simply warns Caucasians for drug use on the job, but for persons of color found using drugs, the business fires them on the spot, this is disparate treatment and illegal discrimination.

Employers also have an obligation to make sure no employees are harassed because of their disability. Jokes made at the expense of a disabled person are actionable as contributing to a hostile work environment when they become pervasive and unwelcome. Once the company is aware of the issues of name calling, wise-cracking, or insults that are perceived as unwelcome, they must remedy the situation immediately. As with all issues, the company must teach and emphasize an environment of equal treatment.

Obesity Versus Morbid Obesity

A woman applies for a job and is turned down because the company states that at 5′2″ tall with a weight of 320 lb she clearly is not fit for the job. The employer cites the Center for Disease Control (CDC) statistics that morbidly obese people miss more time from work and have difficulty with some of the physical requirements that are part of the job; therefore, she will be unable to handle the essential duties of the job.

Taking a group average and applying it to one person within the group is stereotyping. This defense will not hold up in court. The company could have arranged a medical examination to determine the candidate's abilities in regard to the job duties as long as all applicants faced the same medical examination.

The company also argued that morbid obesity is not a protected category, and at the time (prior to 1993) they were correct, but when the employee sued and won the case, new law was made. The court for the first time stated that morbid obesity is a disability since it meets the definition of disability under the ADA (Cook v. Rhode Island Department of Mental Retardation, 10 F.3d 17 [1993]).

This morbid obesity is very different from the obesity problem in our country often cited by the medical community. The Cook court referred to morbid obesity meeting the ADA criteria as opposed to obesity being measured by someone being 20% over the standard Body Mass Index (BMI). The company's decision not to hire the morbidly obese woman because of her disabled status is illegal discrimination because she is in a protected category.

Whenever an employee claims he or she is disabled under the ADA the company has a right to review his or her claim. As noted in the first part of this chapter, the ADA definition is controlling.

Employers are not allowed to use criteria that screen or tend to screen disabled individuals from the workplace. The courts found it was illegal discrimination when an employer used the results of a drug test to eliminate workers who were taking legal prescription drugs for a physical condition when there was no realistic connection between the use of the drug and workplace safety (Bates v. Dura Automotive Systems, Inc. 650 F. Supp. 2d 754 [M.D. Tenn. 2009]).

Furthermore, failing to make reasonable accommodation to those with disabilities to perform their job in the workplace is a violation of the law.

Employers should foster the goal of promoting the inclusion of people with disabilities. To meet this goal, they must educate all staff members to respect and have awareness of disability issues and create an atmosphere that allows employees with disabilities to easily take part in all aspects of company facilities by accommodating their needs.

Sexual Orientation

CHAPTER 15

Sexual orientation was not recognized as a protected category in all states until 2020. Prior to that time, there was no federal law banning discrimination based on sexual orientation in the private sector, leading to inconsistency in the states. The landmark case of Bostock v Clayton County, Georgia, decided June 15, 2020, made sexual orientation a fully protected category in all 50 states (Bostock v Clayton County, Georgia, 590 US ___, 2020).

In Bostock v. Clayton County, Georgia, the employer fired a county employee for "unbecoming conduct" after he began participating in a gay recreational softball league.

The U.S. Supreme Court held in a 6-3 decision that an employer who fires or otherwise discriminates against an individual simply for being gay or transgender does so "because of . . . sex," in violation of Title VII of the Civil Rights Act of 1964. Writing for the majority, Justice Gorsuch, joined by Chief Justice John Roberts and four other Supreme Court Justices, ruled that employers that discriminate against employees based on sexual orientation or gender identity violate federal law.

The court specifically stated: "An employer violates Title VII when it intentionally fires an individual employee based in part on sex. It makes no difference if other factors besides the plaintiff's sex contributed to the decision or that the employer treated women as a group the same when compared to men as a group. A statutory violation occurs if an employer intentionally relies in part on an individual employee's sex when deciding to discharge the employee. Because discrimination on the basis of homosexuality or transgender status requires an employer to intentionally treat individual employees differently because of their sex, an employer who intentionally penalizes an employee for being homosexual or transgender also violates Title VII. There is no escaping the role intent plays: Just as sex is necessarily a but-for cause when an employer discriminates against homosexual or transgender employees, an employer who discriminates on these grounds inescapably intends to rely on sex in its decision-making."

Sexual orientation discrimination refers to differential treatment based on someone's perceived or actual gay, lesbian, bi-sexual, or heterosexual orientation. It is illegal to not hire or fire an employee based on sexual orientation. Furthermore, the illegal discrimination extends to any tangible employment action being based on that status such as being passed over for a promotion, being given baseless warnings or far more stringent goals for improvement.

Gay And Straight Employees Are Protected

It is important to understand that this category protects a person from being fired for being straight as well as being fired for being gay. In addition, actionable harassment includes unwelcome and pervasive comments regarding the employee's sexual orientation as well as tangible employment actions.

Some employers will attempt to defend their right to discriminate based on sexual orientation on the basis of their own religious belief. Stay tuned for these cases landing in various appeals courts around the country.

Prior to the U.S. Supreme Court decision in Bostock, in states where sexual orientation was not protected, an employee could be legally discharged solely for being straight or gay.

Congratulations! There's the door.

Before June 15, 2020 the response to the scenario below was legal.

Tracy has been working for United Leggings for five years. She has been a good employee. One day her supervisor, Ellen, walks by Tracy's desk and stops to notice a new framed picture.

Ellen points at the new photo. "Great picture. Love the frame. It looks so festive and you look so vibrant. What is going on there?"

Tracy proudly says, "I just got married. That is my wedding picture with my wife, Laurie. We tied the knot after living together for over three years. She made an honest woman out of me."

"Congratulations. Where was the picture taken?"

"Oh, we were in St Martin. It was beautiful."

"That is so great. Please tell your bride she is a lucky woman," Ellen says as she shakes Tracy's hand vigorously.

Tracy returns to working on her monthly report when she gets a call to report to human resources and to bring her office manual. She assumes they are adding in a few new policies to the employee handbook. Tracy walks into the human resource director's office, and is promptly fired. She is told that once the company knew she was gay they needed to cut ties with her immediately because, "some of the other employees are just not comfortable working with someone who is gay."

In states that did not recognize sexual orientation as a protected category, this firing of Tracy was legal and just part of the employment at-will status. But as of the summer of 2020, all states recognize sexual orientation as a protected category, and the firing of Tracy would constitute illegal discrimination.

Now that this category is recognized in the United States without exception, all sexual orientations are protected. Consequently, if Jeanette had a picture of her and her new husband, Gus, and was fired for being heterosexual, she would have a case for wrongful termination. This category is not just about protecting gay employees, but all employees and candidates from discrimination based on sexual orientation.

Hiring Issues

During the hiring process if an employer appears to consider the candidate's inclusion in a protected class while making hiring decisions, they will expose the company to liability.

Why Are You Asking That?

An important concept in this area is to never ask a question that has no bearing on the company's final hiring decision. Some inexperienced human resource people get nervous and start asking inane questions that they later try to justify as just getting to know the person. In reality, they were unwittingly laying the groundwork for a potential employment law case.

A classic example is the interviewer asking a job applicant, "So, have you started your Christmas shopping yet?"

It seems like an innocuous question at first glance, but when the applicant responds with, "Oh, I don't celebrate Christmas because I am Muslim," the foundation for a discrimination lawsuit has been laid. The company picks someone else for the job over the Muslim applicant.

The rejected candidate of the Muslim faith claims she was not hired because of her religion. The company vehemently denies that its hiring decision had anything to do with the fact that the employer learned the interviewee was Muslim, yet the litigation commences.

In the district court trial 2 years later, the lawyer for the Muslim applicant continues with her cross-examination of the hiring director who performed the interview and made the final job decision.

"When you were meeting with the plaintiff, Fatima, for the job opening, why did you ask her if she had completed her Christmas shopping?"

"I . . . I . . . I"

"Was that question meant to elicit any information for the purposes of making your decision?"

"No, I was just curious since it was early December. I was just making conversation."

"Really, just making conversation? As an experienced hiring director, don't you plan out your questions?"

"Well, usually, I have some specific questions, but there is some leeway for just getting to know the job seekers better."

"And isn't it true that a question about shopping for Christmas is for you to subtly determine who is a Christian and who is not or in essence to weed out the non-Christians?"

"No, our company does not discriminate."

"Oh, then educate the jury on why you asked that question. Tell us what relevance that question has to working as an accountant in your office!"

"I was just wanting to get to know her better."

"Oh really. It is important to know what religion she is."

There is no good answer to that question. That is the point. If there is no good answer as to why the question was asked, do not ask it.

Most human resource people know from day one on the job that they cannot ask obviously improper questions like, "so what country are your parents from," but so many other poor questions get asked leading to potential problems.

This chapter would go far too long if we listed all the questions that must be avoided such as:

- "Are you planning on having a big family?"
- "How many children do you have?"
- "Are you married or engaged or living with someone?"
- "You have some unusual coloring. What are you? I mean what nationality are you?"
- "You were limping when you came in. Do you have a disability you should tell me about?"
- "How's your health?"
- "What's your religion?"
- "Are you planning on becoming pregnant?"
- "Where were you born?"
- "What arrangements are you able to make for child care while you are at work?"
- "Will you be requesting personal time off for certain holidays?"

Avoid any questions related to potentially eliciting information on protected class status. All interviewers should prepare a list of questions that outline the actual job skills and experience essential for the position to avoid rambling and bringing up topics that have nothing to do with the company's evaluation of the potential employee.

The interview process should be consistent. Asking men and women different types of questions is improper and may give rise to a gender discrimination lawsuit. The courts have even indicated certain lines of questioning may be gender discriminatory such as when an interviewer chats with the two finalists for the job about hunting. The woman applicant says she does not hunt, but the man in his interview shares some classic hunting stories from his past. The company ultimately hires the male candidate over the female claiming the man was just a better fit, leading to a potential claim of gender discrimination.

Do not ask candidates about skills or ability to complete duties that are not contained in the job description. It is not relevant to ask the applicant if he or she can lift more than 60 lb three times per hour if that requirement is not part of the actual duties of the job in question.

A more recent trend in the hiring process is performing an Internet search on the applicant. An Internet search may reveal information related to the applicant's inclusion in a protected category. That search may lead to the employer possessing data that should have nothing to do with the employment action. It can be difficult to later negate a claim that the company did not decide based upon this protected status.

All hiring decisions need to be documented. To be prepared for future claims by rejected job applicants, the company should keep a written record of the hiring process, documenting the reasons for the ultimate hiring decision—reasons that had nothing to do with the applicant's inclusion in a protected category.

It is far easier to defend the decision if the determination was based on test scores, pertinent job experience, and recommendations as opposed to a statement that "we just liked Susan over Olivia because Susan fit in better with the company's personnel."

It is legal to request criminal records and to not hire an applicant based on his or her criminal record. Criminal status based on past criminal acts is not a protected category, and thus, while it is discrimination to not hire any applicants with a criminal record, it is not illegal discrimination.

There is a new movement termed "ban the box" that asks employers to take the question of past criminal arrests, guilty pleas, and convictions off the employment application. The impetus for removing this question in the initial phase of the interview process is to avoid early elimination of the candidate without being able to hear his or her explanation of past issues in person. Laws regarding this question vary by state.

Hiring Errors, Disability, and Medical Examinations

The laws prohibit employers from inquiring about disabilities or conducting medical examinations of prospective employees prior to hiring them. It is illegal to ask questions about medical history, prior worker's compensation claims, or overall health before a hiring decision is made.

The employer, however, is permitted to ask about a candidate's abilities as long as they are specifically related to the essential duties of the position in question. An employer should not ask, "So, are you disabled in any way?" It is, however, appropriate to ask, "Can you lift 15 lb on a regular and repetitive basis," as long as the 15 lb repetitive lifting is a requirement of the job in question.

A company is prohibited from refusing to hire an applicant whose disability makes them unable to perform a nonessential job duty. The question will arise if a particular duty is essential to the job. The company must document this determination.

The employer does have the absolute right to request that the candidate submit to a medical examination, so long as the employer does not pick and choose who must be examined, but demands all prospective employees undergo the same medical inquiry. The company cannot, for example, only demand that male applicants and not female candidates submit to a medical exam.

A company may condition the job offer on the results of the medical examination. In the event the examination evidences that the person would not be able to perform the job's essential functions, even with reasonable accommodation, the company is within its legal right to rescind the offer. Furthermore, if the doctor's report indicates the prospective worker would pose a direct threat to health or safety in the workplace, this would also be sufficient basis for rescinding the offer.

Recruitment

Companies need to be able to prove they complied with all the laws designed to make sure equal opportunity employment is at the core of their hiring policies.

What may appear to be a neutral hiring practice may result in discrimination as evidenced in the EEOC decision from 2016 against defendant FAPS, Inc., a company located at Port Newark, N.J. (EEOC v. FAPS, Inc., C.A. No. 2:10-cv-03095 [D.N.J. June 15, 2016]). In this case, the EEOC alleged that the company engaged in a pattern or practice of race discrimination by relying on word-of-mouth hiring, which resulted in a predominantly white workforce despite the substantial available African-American workforce in the Newark area.

Employers must be able to demonstrate that the recruitment and advertising for employees does not result in discrimination. An advertisement that says the company is looking for "recent college graduates" clearly will discourage the 40 and older crowd from applying. Advertising for the new job opening solely in the Lutheran World Gazette would only reach certain groups, effectively limiting some categories of being aware of the potential hiring.

Several states have enacted laws to stop employers from asking candidates about salary history in a move legislators believe will curtail pay inequity by gender. This idea is based on the premise that asking the question encourages employers to pay the same salary as the employee was paid previously and no more.

This is an issue for people who experience pay disparity already because it can further or continue that disparity even after career changes. The prohibition in regard to asking about prior salary is aimed at disrupting the cycle of wage inequality for women and people of color. Employers would worry less about what a person was paid and look at their qualifications to set the salary.

These laws do not limit employers from making statements about the anticipated salary, bonus, and benefits for a position. In addition, companies can ask applicants about their expectations or requirements for salary, benefits, bonus, or commission structure.

As discussed earlier, questions that elicit information leading to knowledge of inclusion in a protected category such as, "What year were you born" should be eliminated from all applications. Consequently, all application forms should be reviewed to remove any questions that have no bearing on choosing the candidate. A company must be able to defend and justify each question, even those contained in the preprinted standard form. And do not assume that just because the questionnaire was found on the Internet, it is acceptable.

A company's defense of, "Oh that question about the applicant's marital status was already in the form, and we never really looked at it," will not play well for the jury.

In regard to age discrimination, advertising for job openings may give rise to a subtler form of bias when the wording discourages older candidates from applying. One ad said, "Company seeks applicant with 3 to 7 years (no more than 7 years) of relevant experience." This language may have a disparate impact on older applicants.

Affirmative Action

The legal fly in the employment law ointment is affirmative action. Affirmative action is a program or set of guidelines instituted to advance qualified minorities and give more opportunities for historically excluded categories of persons. Affirmative action policies usually focus on providing underrepresented groups, such as women and minorities, equal access to employment to remedy for past discrimination and prevent future discrimination.

Affirmative action is meant to rectify centuries of social, racial, and economic oppression. But opponents argue that giving an advantage to one group creates a disadvantage to other groups. Further, there is no question that when the employer uses an affirmative action policy to recruit, hire, promote, and embrace diversity, they are making decisions based on someone's inclusion in a protected category. That is a definition of employment discrimination.

Some say merit should be the only criteria in the employment realm, but conversely many say it should be a proactive effort to reach out and employ groups that have faced hurdles, glass ceilings, and discrimination.

The best affirmative action policy does not discuss quotas or targets, but outlines plans and efforts designed to ensure that people who belong to minority groups receive equal opportunity and fair treatment and are not subject to discrimination as well as aggressive recruitment efforts to make minorities aware of the company's opportunities. Quotas are inflexible and predeterminative of numbers as opposed to something an employer can strive toward (University of California v. Bakke, 438 U.S. 265 [1978]).

Drug Testing

Employees seeking first-time employment can be tested as a condition of employment, even if there is no cause or reason to believe that the prospective employee has been taking drugs. The employer, however, must test all incoming employees for drugs, not just certain candidates. A candidate has a right to refuse the drug test, but the employer can legally refuse to hire them based on the refusal.

Employers need to make sure that if they are adopting a policy of drug testing current employees, the test is not based on an applicant's or employee's inclusion in a protected category. A company cannot only drug test the male candidates and not the female ones. A company should have a well-written drug policy listing all substances tested for and consequences if there is a positive result from the test. The policy should have clear definitions of all terms used to avoid ambiguity and should contain a section addressing prescription drugs, including medical marijuana. Drug testing can be very expensive; the cost needs to be considered as part of the equation.

Random drug testing is a tool employers often utilize to deter drug and alcohol use in the workplace. When a company says the drug testing is random, the method used to select the people being tested better, indeed, be random, and there must be documentation to demonstrate that the method to select candidates for drug testing is arbitrary.

Employees can also be tested based on suspicion, but again, if it appears the employer tends to be "suspicious" of only certain protected groups, this will be scrutinized and will lead to a viable claim of discrimination. It is important to have training for management personnel to recognize signs of drug use and abuse.

Instead of drug testing based on suspicion, when the company notes that the employee's work is suffering, they can directly address the diminished quality of the employee's work. A conference with the employee would be indicated to warn them that unless they improve their job performance within a very short time frame their job is in jeopardy. As discussed earlier, the written warning must be unambiguous.

It is imperative that the employer does not differentiate on how they will proceed based on any protected categories; the employer must document all actions to prove all policies were followed.

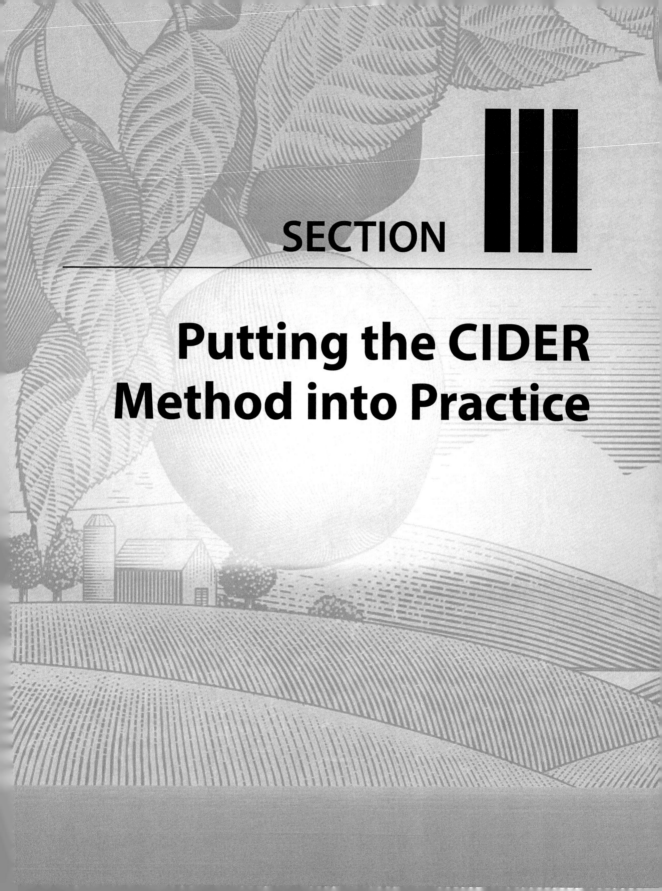

SECTION III

Putting the CIDER Method into Practice

The Fun Begins: Using the CIDER Method to Handle Employee Complaints

CHAPTER 17

N ow that the reader is keenly aware of the employment laws and the necessity of companies utilizing the CIDER method to properly handle all complaints, it is time to put all of this knowledge into practice.

Each and every employee complaint will be handled systematically without worrying that some random supervisor will unilaterally decide to simply tell that kidder Bob to try to pick his targets for sexy sweater ranking a bit more carefully.

The foundation of proper communication skills and investigation acumen combined with understanding employment law has prepared the reader to begin properly, analyzing and investigating employee complaints. The format of Communicate, Investigate, Document, Evaluate, Respond, and Follow-up is the basis of the entire process.

This section of the book contains sample employee complaints to study and scrutinize while applying the lessons previously learned. In Chapters Seventeen to Twenty, the reader will follow and observe the process since all the steps in the CIDER method are outlined in depth. As the book winds down, however, the responsibility for analyzing and handling the investigation will increasingly fall to the reader. In Chapters Twenty-one and Twenty-two, the reader will be doing the heavy lifting of completing the majority of the steps of the investigation.

Once a company has fully implemented the CIDER method, employee complaints will not go to a random manager but to the specific person handpicked and trained for this important position.

Sexual Harassment Complaint

For this complaint, Avery is the employee designated within the corporation to whom employees will make their complaints. She has been trained in the nuances of communication (Chapter Two) and all aspects of the CIDER method. She has practiced the application of the skills and is ready to handle this job.

Steve Jones knocks on Avery's door and says, "Do you have a few minutes?"

Avery closes her laptop and says, "Of course I have time. Come on in and shut the door."

COMMUNICATE: Avery grabs her pen and pad. She leans forward in her chair (because leaning forward conveys interest) as Steve sits down across from her.

© Tyler Olson/Shutterstock.com

Steve looks around like he is about to give the nuclear codes and begins. "You know Susan Fishman in bookkeeping? Well she is coming on to me . . . big time."

Now this is a real test for Avery since Steve looks like he hit the wall years ago . . . and the wall fell on him. He is dull, arrogant, and slow (a triple threat). Susan is brilliant, and Avery cannot imagine a world in which Susan would have any interest in Steve.

She stops the impulse to roll her eyes and asks, "When did this start?"

Avery's body language evidences interest and conveys that she wants to hear every detail. She has also been taught not to offer any evaluations or comments that could be construed as negative or positive and might inhibit communication.

Avery takes copious notes as Steve goes on for 45 minutes about how Susan is really making a play for him. At the conclusion of the interview, she asks Steve to listen as she reads back the detailed notes to see if he has any corrections or additions. In the event he wants to expand or revisit a topic, Avery will not only allow it but encourage it.

Avery informs Steve that the company will be investigating his complaint and asks him not to discuss his concerns with other workers to avoid hampering the investigation. She formalizes the summary of the interview to document the meeting. Subsequently, Avery asks Steve to come to her office to read and execute the typed memorandum verifying its accuracy. If he has any changes, no matter how incidental, they will be made promptly. After finalizing the detailed synopsis of Steve's complaint, Avery writes down her impressions to aid her recollection of Steve's demeanor and credibility to be able to elaborate on her assessment of each witness during the evaluation phase of the CIDER method.

INVESTIGATE: Avery meets with the supervisor of the CIDER process, Donna, to review the complaint and outline a plan for a thorough investigation. The supervisor reviews both Susan and Steve's personnel files to see if there are any prior similar issues. If Steve's file contains a record of him making 10 previous unsubstantiated complaints against other employees, his credibility would be taken into consideration as part of the evaluation phase. If Susan's file shows a history of similar issues filed by other employees, this is very germane to deciding the company's response.

The supervisor reports that there is nothing in either personnel file that is relevant to the present complaint. She directs Avery to interview Susan within the next business day utilizing the questions they crafted together to make sure the interview goes to the heart of the issues. Donna also asks that Avery speak with any employees who work near Steve and Susan. She reminds Avery to prepare a complete written account of their meeting as well as all future conferences which will include each item discussed and decided as part of the documentation.

At 10:00 am the next day Susan comes to Avery's office for the meeting. When she closes the door, Susan asks, "Am I in trouble?"

"Susan, as you are aware from our company meetings, whenever a complaint is filed we investigate. The fact that we are investigating does not mean we have made any evaluation. It simply means we are doing our due diligence as we do with every complaint," Avery replies.

"So, someone complained about me?"

"A complaint was filed by Steve Jones claiming you are making him feel uncomfortable with unwanted attention that he feels is sexual in nature. The complaint was received by our office yesterday, and I am responsible for investigating the matter."

"Me and Steve, sexual?"

"Steve says you are constantly staring at him."

"I mean maybe I have looked at him when he wears one of his crazy bow ties."

"Do you talk to him about any nonwork-related issues?"

Susan replies, "Sure, but real innocuous stuff like, is that a new bow tie or does that bow tie have an off switch."

Avery is not just writing bullet points but setting forth the full version of Steve's comments. "Have you ever indicated you would like to see him outside of work?"

"Heavens no."

"Even in a kidding manner?"

Susan rolls her eyes and says, "Oh my goodness. I mean I probably have said something like, 'I would love to come with you to watch you pick out those bow ties to see if you are simply throwing a dart or intentionally picking them.'"

"Has Steve ever told you that you make him uncomfortable?"

Susan sighs and says, "He asked me to quit commenting on his clothes."

"Did you stop when he asked?"

"It's just some good-natured kidding. I thought he liked the attention."

The inquiry continues to explore Susan's recollections of their interactions. Avery asks Susan to listen carefully while she reads back the notes outlining the conversation. Susan says she wants to talk to Steve to clear the air. Avery asks her not to have that conversation until the company has completed the investigation. Avery types up her detailed notes and obtains Susan's signature verifying the accuracy of the memorandum.

The supervisor reviews the investigation with Avery and determines that Debbie Sizemore must be interviewed since her desk is between Steve and Susan's office. Avery commences the meeting with Debbie and recites the preamble about the company's promise to investigate every complaint and that the inquiry does not in any way indicate the company has made a determination of misconduct. Debbie is hesitant to say anything negative because she really likes Susan. Debbie acknowledges that she has heard Susan kid Steve about his clothes, saying, "I mean I have heard her make a few slams about his bow-tie choices."

Avery asks if Debbie has seen any behavior from Susan that is sexual in nature toward Steve or any comments that she thinks could be interpreted as sexual attention. "Absolutely not," Debbie states.

Debbie listens intently as Avery reads back the notes. She says she remembers one other thing. After Susan was giving Steve some guff about his new bow tie, "Steve told me, no one would focus on my clothes that much if they weren't deeply into me. I just assumed Steve was making a joke cuz there is no way he could think Susan is into him that way."

DOCUMENT: Avery copies the three interview summaries for the meeting with Donna; they are typed with quotes and executed by the employees (Steve, Susan, and Debbie) confirming the contents as accurate. It is also Avery's responsibility to carefully and thoroughly document the meeting with Donna (the supervisor) including the evaluation and responses considered and ultimately chosen.

EVALUATE: The supervisor feels that the amount of investigation is sufficient and that no additional interviews or research is required to have a solid basis for reaching a conclusion. After reviewing all the investigative material, Donna determines that Susan was not sexually harassing Steve. However, Susan's comments, while not sexual in nature, should have stopped when Steve made it clear he was not enjoying the bantering.

RESPONSE: The supervisor, with input from Avery, considers several options as potential responses based on the findings. Some of the alternatives considered, but not chosen include sensitivity training for Susan, moving Susan's office to the other end of the building, and moving Steve's office. The supervisor determines that the best solution is to give Susan a written warning to restrict her comments with Steve to business related issues only and to refrain from any further critiques of Steve's clothing.

Donna asks Avery to meet with Steve and advise him that the company is ordering Susan to immediately stop all comments relating to his attire. She will also emphasize that based on the investigation the company found that Susan's behavior toward Steve was not sexual in nature.

The details of the meeting are outlined by Avery in the evaluation report, including the alternatives that the company considered and rejected, together with the reasons for those decisions. Avery sets up meetings with Susan and Steve. Donna prepares a memo outlining the company's reprimand to Susan to give her as part of the meeting. Avery will have Susan sign the copy to acknowledge receipt of the original.

The meetings go well, although Steve is insistent that Susan was coming on to him, and the company is taking her side. Avery explains that it was important that he alerted the company of his concerns and assures him that she believes he will have no further issues with Susan, but if he does, he should immediately contact her (Avery).

FOLLOW-UP: One month after implementing the response, Avery meets with Steve to review the matter. The meeting is not casual, but a formal, scheduled conference to convey that the company takes the entire process very seriously.

Steve says he is satisfied that his grievances were addressed and says Susan is no longer coming on to him, staring at him, or commenting on his clothes, but he again makes his case that she was coming on to him previously. Avery drafts a memo documenting the meeting. The memo will be placed in Steve and Susan's personnel files with the other memos and investigation findings.

I Want to Save His Soul

The next employee complaint should set off far more alarms as compared to the Steve and Susan scenario from Chapter Seventeen. For the purpose of the example, Oscar is the company's primary individual whom employees are urged to contact when they have a grievance. The business also has a designated back-up employee to hear complaints in the event Oscar is unavailable or the employee is uncomfortable discussing the complaint with the primary person. Oscar has been trained and has held this position for over 5 years.

I Want to Save His Soul

David walks into Oscar's office and says, "I hope I'm in the right place. I remember from some meeting that you're the one I am supposed to come to with a complaint, right?"

COMMUNICATE: Oscar immediately puts aside what he is working on and says, "Absolutely. Please sit down and tell me what's on your mind," as he grabs a pen and a legal pad. He has been taught and knows it is far more conducive to communication to take notes in writing as opposed to on the computer.

"You know Dwayne Robertson who works next to me? Well he keeps asking me why I don't believe in Jesus, and do I know I'm going to hell because I don't.

"I would deflect the first few times he brought it up, but he is relentless. He's bringing me pamphlets, sending me emails and keeps stopping by my desk to tell me how worried he is about my soul. He asked if I realized Jesus was Jewish like I am and that he died for my sins. This morning he left this crucifix on my desk." David slides the crucifix across the desk.

David goes on for another 5 minutes with additional examples. Oscar takes detailed notes, and when David stops, he asks open-ended questions such as, "What other conversations can you recall?" and "Who else is around when Dwayne brings this topic up to you?"

David responds, "Now he's bringing in reinforcements. He had Denise and Alberto with him yesterday. They are both part of Dwayne's prayer group. Denise tells me if I accept Jesus as my savior, my life will be so much better, and the office staff wouldn't think of me as an outsider. Who knew I was thought of as an outsider?

"Alberto asked me why Jews don't believe in God. I told them I do not want to have any more religious discussions, but they just will not stop or even slow down. Dwayne kept badgering me about if I believe in God. I told him Jews do believe in God just not Jesus Christ. He said that is absurd, since you cannot have one without the other.

"Denise was supposed to turn in her report to me yesterday on the focus group's view of our new packaging. So, I go to her office and tell her the report is overdue, and she said 'good luck in hell,' and held up her cross in my direction."

The meeting lasts until David says he has voiced all his concerns. Oscar asks David to listen carefully as he reads back the notes to make sure they are 100% accurate. Oscar requests that David not talk to anyone at work about his complaint to avoid affecting the upcoming investigation. As soon as David leaves, Oscar types the notes since he has been taught to formalize the conversation as soon as possible to limit errors and gaps as time dulls the recollection of specifics.

Later in the day, Oscar brings David the typed summary to review and sign. While David is reviewing the typed version he says, "These are good except that I forgot to tell you that someone is leaving a daily prayer on my desk that starts out, 'There is no heaven without Jesus.'" Oscar returns to his office revising the notes to incorporate the additional information and obtain David's signature, stating the notes are accurate and complete.

INVESTIGATE: Oscar sets up a meeting with the supervisor, Betsy, to map out the investigation, which entails interviewing the parties David mentioned plus other employees who may be aware of these conversations. Betsy says to meet with Dwayne first and then Denise and Alberto in no particular order, but she wants those three interviewed in the next two business days.

Oscar arranges for Dwayne to come to his office for an interview and recites the important preamble that is said to each interviewee. "Dwayne, as you know from our meetings it is our office policy to investigate each and every complaint we receive. The fact that we are investigating does not in any way mean we have determined the complaint has validity but simply means we are following our protocol to look into any concern raised by a company employee."

Dwayne's smile leaves his face and he slumps in the chair. "Is this about me or . . ."

"David Hoffberg filed a grievance stating that you have made him feel uncomfortable with the ongoing discussions of religion."

Dwayne comes to life and sits up straight, "No way! Have they rescinded the First Amendment while I wasn't looking? I mean has religious freedom packed up and left for Canada? I am trying to save a guy from eternal damnation. I think that is a lot more important than, well . . . just about anything."

Oscar has learned that it is crucial at this point to not engage Dwayne or directly respond to his argumentative questions since Dwayne may infer an opinion as to the issues. This is the time to obtain his side of the story. Oscar is well aware that if he argues, challenges, or even comments, that may limit the interviewee's willingness to tell all the details from his perspective. Oscar asks, "Tell me more about what you and David talk about?"

"Well I have said lots of stuff to him, but I also ask him a lot of questions to understand his viewpoint. You see, I like David and knowing he is going to hell for not accepting Jesus as his savior really upsets me."

"Tell me some specific religious conversations you have had with David."

"Ok. Like yesterday I asked him if he knew Jesus was Jewish. Then I wanted to know if he believes in God. He said yes, but he does not believe in Jesus. I said, 'Don't you care that you will not go to heaven when you die?'"

"Has David ever told you he does not want to discuss this topic?"

"I suppose he has, but this is too important to ignore. Don't I owe it to someone to try and save them?"

"When he asked you to . . ."

"Wait a second; I want you to answer my question. Don't you believe it a duty of every person to help another?"

"Dwayne, my objective today is to try to get your side of what has been going on. That is my job, and anything else is contrary to that goal. Have any other employees been present when you are discussing your views with David?"

"These are not my views; these are the facts as set forth in the New Testament. Some of the time I have talked with David, and a few people from the prayer group were present; Denise, Alberto, and I think Judi."

"Judi Thomas the supervisor?"

"Yeah, she organizes the prayer group."

The meeting goes on for another 40 minutes and Dwayne's version of the conversations is very similar to what David said. When Oscar is convinced there is no additional information to obtain, he thanks him for his time and asks him to listen as he reads back his notes to make sure they are accurate.

Dwayne says, "Do you believe in free speech?" At this point it is crucial Oscar emphasizes that his opinions are not relevant, and his job is to accurately obtain Dwayne's recollection of all the events and conversations that are germane to the complaint.

Oscar tells Dwayne he will type up the notes and ask him to carefully read them to cross-check their completeness and sign each page to verify that they are accurate.

The next phase of the investigation entails meeting with Denise. Oscar begins the conference with the same preamble as he gave Dwayne and that he uses before meeting with any interviewees prior to addressing the specifics of the topic.

"Denise, do you have any recollection of talking to David Hoffberg about religion?'

"I sure do. There were a few of us trying to keep him from going to hell. The odd dichotomy is he is one of the chosen people cuz he's a Jew, but he will go to hell if he does not accept Christ. I am not very comfortable working with heathens. I really tried my best to help him see the light, but he doesn't seem to care about it. I really have now washed my hands of him and his lack of faith."

Denise goes on, "I talk to lots of other employees about religion and abortion and no one else minds, and last I checked, it is a free country."

Eventually Oscar asks Denise, "Do you recall a conversation when David asked you about the status of your report on the focus group's impressions on the new packaging?"

Denise looks at the floor and says, "I didn't think that was his business to criticize me."

"I am just trying to learn about all the discussions you two have had about religion. Whatever you can remember would be really helpful."

"I can't remember everything I said. I was mad. But I know I have told him several times if he does not wake up and accept Jesus Christ, he is going to hell."

The interview proceeds another 15 minutes. Oscar asks Denise to listen as he reads back the notes. Approximately 2 hours later he brings the formalized interview summary to Denise to read and sign confirming the accuracy of the contents.

Oscar contacts Alberto and initiates his interview with the same introductory language to emphasize the company is not accusing, but simply investigating. Oscar asks about his conversations with David regarding religion. Alberto gets very animated, "Is it that Mexicans are not allowed to speak their mind? Ya know, my friends keep asking if the company treats me the same as everybody else, and I defend this place, but I guess I was just being a stupid Mexican."

This a real challenge for Oscar not to react to Alberto's words since Oscar knows this interview is not motivated by anything but obtaining detailed statements from the parties David named.

"Alberto, I am just compiling information in regard to a complaint that was made."

"Why don't you talk to Denise or Dwayne, or is it that they aren't minorities?"

This is a tough spot since Oscar would like to say he has talked to them, but that may violate the confidential nature of the investigation. Oscar does state that, as part of every investigation, he meets with all parties who have been identified in any complaint raised.

Alberto seems to calm down, and he uncrosses his arms.

"I talk to David and lots of employees about a lot of stuff. I don't keep notes of everything I say."

"I understand that. We are just trying to find out what you remember about any religious conversations that you had with David."

"I have never talked to David one on one. It was always with Dwayne. Dwayne asked me to help him save a good guy. I guess he's not that good a guy if he's trying to get us in trouble by reporting us. Do I need a lawyer?"

"We are just asking you to tell us what you remember about these talks. We are not cross-examining or questioning anything you say but only wanting to get all the information available."

"You know, all I hear about is how America is a place of freedom of expression. I express that believing in Jesus is the pathway to heaven, and here I am in trouble."

The meeting goes on for a total of 30 minutes and Oscar lets Alberto know that he will be asking him to execute the formalized notes to confirm they completely represent all he said.

The supervisor directs Oscar to also interview Judi Thomas in light of Dwayne's statement indicating she was present for one of the religious conversations. Oscar is more nervous about interviewing her as she has been with the company for many years and is upper management. Oscar, however, begins the meeting in the same manner he has been taught, easing into the interview and letting Ms. Thomas know this is standard procedure whenever a complaint is received.

Judi says she has a vague recollection of walking by Dwayne and Denise talking to David. "Dwayne stopped me and said, 'Don't you think David should come to one of the prayer meetings you organize?' I told David we would love to have him at a prayer meeting and that we meet every Wednesday morning before work in the office conference room on second floor."

"Did you ever talk to David about believing in Jesus?"

"I told him he would really enjoy the meetings because we are all celebrating our belief, and it is so joyful."

The meeting with Ms. Thomas ends after 15 minutes. Oscar tells her he will stop by her office to have her read and sign the final version of his notes to confirm they are accurate.

DOCUMENT: Oscar has the typed memoranda outlining the full text of each interview with David, Alberto, Denise, and Judi executed by the employees stating the information contained in the summaries is accurate and complete. The supervisor (Betsy) requests copies of the statements to review in preparation for the evaluation meeting.

Oscar knows it will be his responsibility to document the conclusions reached and alternatives considered for responding to the complaint stemming from the evaluation conference. The detailed evaluation report must also include copies of any research or information used in considering, analyzing, and deciding the issues.

EVALUATE: It is crucial to identify all the concerns that the complaint and subsequent investigation has raised, including free speech, religious freedom and the prayer meetings. The company must recognize the potential issues if it is to make a fair and accurate evaluation. Without conducting a just and complete evaluation, a business cannot respond appropriately.

It is important to research past EEOC rulings on this topic prior to completing an investigation to better understand applicable case law. Prior EEOC rulings have indicated that discussion (including religious discussion) directed toward employees by coworkers and managers may constitute harassment if it is abusive or persists after the employees to whom it is directed have made it clear that it is unwelcome. (Both employees and employers can contact the EEOC directly with questions.)

It is clear that a private company has the right to limit and regulate speech, even political and religious conversations, when the speech interferes with business. Calling the conversation a debate does not make it acceptable.

In making any decision, the company must be sure that it conveys that religious freedom is crucial to the working environment. But it is proper to distinguish the faithful practice of each employee's religion, including styles of dress or wearing a cross, from trying to recruit others to their denomination or denigrating another faith. An employee having a poster saying Jesus Saves on their desk is not the same as continuing to advocate for religion after one employee has asked other employees to stop.

Religious freedom is differentiated from unwelcome speech. Each employee is free to believe as he or she chooses, but constant talk when an employee has made it clear they do not wish to discuss the subject further likely constitutes harassment.

The investigation showed that the conversations in question were unwelcome, harassing, and disruptive to the business. Further, it was not one isolated incident, but the conversations were pervasive. Allowing the continuing conduct in light of the circumstances could manifest into unlawful religious harassment.

When coworkers harass an employee on the basis of his or her faith to the point of creating an abusive or intimidating work environment, it may constitute discrimination under a hostile work environment theory. Thus, a simple disagreement over religious principles would probably not constitute unlawful harassment; but if the conversations are pervasive, and if the communications could be found to harass or intimidate an employee on the basis of religion, that may cross the line of lawful conduct. The employer is culpable if made aware of the communications that might constitute illegal harassment but fails to rectify the situation. Consequently, an immediate response is necessary to remedy this matter.

After reviewing the EEOC information and examining all of the employee statements, the supervisor, Betsy, concludes that the company is within its authority to demand that the employees named stop discussing religion with David since the religious advocacy was persistent and unwelcome.

The findings from the investigation have made it evident that the company must intervene and correct this situation as well as making sure no other similar problems are simmering in the company.

The evaluation, including the consideration of the importance of first amendment issues, must be documented. Betsy is confident that ordering the employees to cease and desist from discussing religion with David is not violating the employee's freedom of religion or freedom of speech or suppressing religious expression in the workplace.

A further inquiry, however, must be made concerning Alberto's insinuation that he was being targeted because of his national origin. Betsy asks that Oscar again meet with Alberto to determine if he has any other concerns of unequal treatment based on national origin.

The investigation also flushed out another underlying issue that must be addressed—the potential problems of a supervisor conducting prayer meetings in the company conference room. There is viability for a claim by an employee to feel pressured to attend in light of a supervisor organizing a prayer group on company property. Consequently, further investigation is necessary to examine if there is any favoritism being shown to those in attendance of the past prayer meetings, not only by Judi Thomas, but by the company in any manner.

Although supervisors retain the same right to religious expression as their employees, supervisors must not be perceived as using their authority to require or discourage religious expression among their employees.

There is no question that organized faith-based assemblies are a minefield for possible claims of religious discrimination. A question that must be answered: is it worth the potential problems to continue to look the other way when worship services are taking place on company property because that indicates company endorsement? Prayer groups in the workplace are not necessarily unlawful, but the company needs to carefully consider the ramifications and determine the best course of action.

Oscar will document the evaluation conference by carefully drafting a well-organized evaluation report that specifically addresses all issues considered and clearly articulates that the company has considered all the evidence. All of the information compiled as part of the investigation as well as detailed summaries of all conferences must be referenced and attached to the report. Oscar will also list the alternatives considered as a response in addition to the company's ultimate resolution.

RESPONSE: The company orders that all religious conversations with David by Dwayne, Denise, and Alberto must stop immediately. Meetings are scheduled with each employee to outline the company's position. They are given written warnings to sign acknowledging their understanding and confirming receipt. The signed warning goes in their respective personnel file, and they keep a copy.

Furthermore, Denise's unreasonable and aggressive response toward David must be dealt with since her reaction was based on her disapproval of his religious beliefs. She will be asked to attend sensitivity training regarding religious tolerance and acceptance within the next 4 weeks as a condition of her continued employment. It was determined that Denise's discomfort working with what she called "heathen" in no way compromised her religious beliefs.

The separate meetings with Dwayne, Denise, and Alberto are simply the first step. The company will also arrange two in-depth conferences. The first session will include all staff and will disseminate the company's position with regard to religious and political expression. The individual running this seminar will stress the need for sensitivity and respect toward others regarding religious beliefs.

The trainings will also address questions on religious diversity and unwelcome speech. It is important to let the employees know they are empowered to say to another employee, "Thank you for your concern, but I am not interested in your church or being saved," and that the message must be understood and respected.

A second educational meeting will be for management level employees to review all forms of anti-harassment/anti-discrimination laws as well as the company's zero tolerance for retaliation. The meeting will also teach supervisors to recognize the disruption that religious expression in the workplace may cause and remind employees in positions of authority to avoid religious conversations or discussions with their subordinates.

With regard to the prayer meetings, the CEO will address all the workers in both training seminars that attendance for any religious meeting has no effect, positive or negative, on an employee's evaluation or prospects for advancement. The CEO will emphasize that if any employee feels pressured to attend the meetings, he or she should file a complaint immediately.

It shall be made clear that it is prohibited to make notes or record of employee attendance at any prayer meetings, and the facilitator of the sessions will stress that the company is not endorsing the prayer meetings.

The company decides that Judi Thomas, as upper-level management, should not lead or organize the meetings, although she can attend and may even speak on occasion. The meeting with Ms. Thomas will outline the company's policies and ask her to sign a document acknowledging the company policy regarding management and prayer meetings.

In addition, the prayer meetings will no longer be allowed on company property, but the employees may use an employer provided bulletin board to invite employees so long as the same bulletin board may be utilized by any employee led groups of a religious nature.

Betsy asks Oscar to meet with David to go over the company's response and ask him to report any further unwelcome religious conversations.

The staff meetings as outlined above are held. An expert in religious dialogue is hired to run both meetings; one for the entire staff and one for management only. Each employee is given a summary of the main points of the meeting and asked to sign a document confirming their attendance. Role playing with employees in situations to better understand the concerns is part of the staff meeting to better help address, outline, and explain the issues. The CEO speaks briefly to show full support of the policies.

FOLLOW-UP: Two to ten weeks after meeting with all parties it is imperative the company's designated representative meet with David to make sure his concerns have been rectified and that no further problems have occurred.

Oscar is assigned that duty. During that follow-up meeting 4 weeks later David reports that since the response to his complaint, several employees have treated him rudely insinuating his actions made Denise quit.

David specifically says, "I have had several employees tell me if I had not been such a whining little crybaby, Denise would still be here and they wouldn't have to go to Denny's two miles away for their prayer meetings."

He also says he is being treated like an outcast since several employees will not talk to him about anything. He stated Ms. Thomas has not treated him differently, but Alberto and Dwayne shun him.

Oscar diplomatically asks David why he did not inform him of these issues earlier. David replies, "And say what? The kids won't play nice with me? I thought if I file any more complaints, no one here will talk to me."

Oscar meets with the CIDER supervisor to discuss the concerns that surfaced in the follow-up interview with David. Is it a form of retaliation if coworkers ignore David? The meeting with David indicates that the poor treatment is only from coworkers and not management.

The supervisor (Betsy) wants to have an additional investigation to discover if the coworkers are getting their cues from any management for their treatment of David.

There is no law that a company must make sure all employees treat their co-employees as friends, but the company must always carefully scrutinize if a protected category status is the cause of the mistreatment or harassment. Betsy and Oscar must consider if the treatment is disruptive to the business or prevents David from doing his job.

Oscar's additional investigation reveals that Alberto and Dwayne are treating David poorly because they feel betrayed and angry and not because they are getting any message from management.

The supervisor outlines various options for responding to the follow-up information. One alternative is seeing this as a no-win situation and offering David a severance package of $60,000.00 (sixty thousand dollars) to sign an agreement giving up any and all potential claims against the company including, but not limited to religious discrimination, harassment, and gender discrimination. Another alternative is to fire Alberto and Dwayne, as they are the instigators of the poor treatment of David. Since the employees are "At-Will" employees, no reason need be given, but they will likely bring a claim for religious discrimination. Although the company is confident they could successfully defend that lawsuit, it would result in attorney fees.

Moving the employees to other locations is another potential option. Doing nothing is always a choice, but in this case, it does not seem like a good choice. Betsy asks Oscar if there are other options that would be responsive. Oscar suggests confining all the parties in a room together and not let them out until they get along. Betsy says that idea tends to blow up, but says having them all work with a counselor who specializes in religious sensitivity training is another alternative to consider.

Betsy determines that a consultation with an employment law attorney is necessary to formulate the best response. She directs Oscar to contact the EEOC directly to get input from their staff concerning the various issues uncovered and their recommended responses.

Each aspect of the process must be documented in-depth. Betsy asks Oscar to meet with her and the employment attorney to maximize his learning. She reminds Oscar to bring all the investigation and additional questions to the consultation. Betsy does not want to unreasonably delay implementing the final response. Consequently, she uploads the investigation materials and forwards those to the attorney for immediate review to expedite the matter. The company will hold off on taking final action in regard to David, Alberto, and Dwayne until the consultation the following day with the attorney.

They Won't Ask Me to Join Them for Lunch

The example from Chapter Eighteen went through each element in-depth to help the reader see the importance of examining all points of view with a wide field of vision. The employee complaints continue, but now the reader takes on more responsibility for analyzing, recognizing, and evaluating the issues as part of the CIDER method.

Joanne walks into Walker's office to report her grievance pursuant to the company's policy for properly registering complaints.

COMMUNICATE: Joanne sits down and says, "I am so upset and know that I am supposed to make the company aware of any unwelcome behavior and, well . . . this is so beyond unwelcome."

Walker stops what he is doing and gets up to close the door. He pulls out his notebook and prepares to make a detailed record of the meeting as per the CIDER training and policies.

Walker: "Tell me what is going on."

Joanne: "I work on a team with Dale, Angie, Mukhtar, Porcha and Chad. Most of them go out to lunch together several days a week and go out after work for drinks every Friday, but they don't ever ask me to join them. I mean never. I even went so far as to tell them I wanted to go with them after work and they just said, 'maybe another time.' I feel horrible and unwelcome."

Walker: "How long has this been going on?"

Joanne: "The first day I was moved to the team, I joined them for lunch and then went out for drinks that Friday. We had a blast. I mean F.U.N., but that was the last time they asked me, and that was 2 months ago. Honestly, I think they have their quota of women in the group, and they don't want me because of my sex."

Walker: "How do the group members treat you during the work on your team projects?"

Joanne: "They are very businesslike and professional, but away from work they act like I have the plague."

The meeting between Walker and Joanne continues for 10 more minutes. Walker reads back his detailed report of all that was covered to confirm the notes are error free.

He subsequently obtains Joanne's signature on the typed memorandum containing a full account of the meeting.

INVESTIGATE: Walker schedules a meeting with his supervisor, Peggy, to review the complaint. Peggy asks that Walker meet with each of the other five members of the team one at a time. They review the approach Walker will take in questioning the other employees. Peggy asks that the interviews be completed within the next 2 days starting with the team leader, Dale.

Walker asks Dale to come to his office for a meeting. When Dale enters, Walker shuts the door and begins his standard explanation that, pursuant to company policy, all complaints are investigated promptly. Walker emphasizes that no judgment has been made, but only that Dale's version of the events needs to be understood to properly evaluate the complaint that has been filed.

> *Walker:* "Dale, I want to ask you about Joanne, who is a member of your team. I assume you know her from your work together."
>
> *Dale:* "Sure, I know her very well. Joanne is a good worker. Her views and creativity really are a nice contribution to our team."
>
> *Walker:* "Joanne is concerned that you and your group seem to exclude her from social get-togethers."
>
> *Dale:* "Oh. She is a bit of a square peg in the round hole on the social side of things. We did ask her to join us after work during her first week with the group and it was just painful. It was like watching a train wreck."
>
> *Walker:* "Can you elaborate on that."
>
> *Dale:* "Do I have to?"
>
> *Walker:* "It is really important to help the company understand what is going on."
>
> *Dale:* "So, our team hangs together a lot outside of work. We have lots of fun when we go out. We stay loose and kid each other and just relax, but Joanne being there just changed everything. She would keep running to each of us and taking selfies and yelling about how much fun she was having. Then she kept asking the waitstaff to take pictures and would scream 'BFF forever!' It was horrible."
>
> *Walker:* "Does your reluctance to include her have anything to do with her being a woman?"
>
> *Dale:* "Our team is made up of men and women. The reason we don't want her is, well, she makes crazy comments . . . like that we don't invite her cuz she is a woman and that kind of crap. It is like she thinks she is Ms. Fun, but she is really Ms. Buzzkill."

The meeting goes on for 5 more minutes until Walker is convinced he has obtained all the relevant information. He explains he may have some follow-up over the next day or two. Dale asks him if he is going to be forced to include Joanne in future outings. Walker explains that he is just compiling information and no evaluation will be made until the investigation is completed. Walker asks Dale to not discuss these concerns with the other team members until the investigation is complete.

Walker brings in another team member, Angie, and goes through the preamble that is always at the front end of the interview. He questions Angie about the concerns that Joanne raised to determine her views on the issues. Walker also asks some pointed questions to see if Dale, as the leader, may be pressuring the others on the team to exclude Joanne.

> *Angie:* "Joanne is oppressive. No one wants to be with her outside of work. She is fine at work, but outside it is like being with a nutjob. I know we should invite her when we go out, but it just isn't a . . . well, frankly, it's horrible. I mean we all get along great and love to kid each other, well, except for Joanne. She is a stick in the mud."
>
> *Walker:* "What do you mean by a stick in the mud?"
>
> *Angie:* "Well not a real stick in the real mud, but someone who single-handedly can destroy an evening. When we did go out with her it was like fingernails on a blackboard. On the one hand she is screaming that she has never had so much fun but then is correcting or apologizing for everything we say."
>
> *Walker:* "Can you give me some specifics from the last time you went out?"
>
> *Angie:* "I call Mukhtar my cute curry eater. He laughs, everyone laughs, but Joanne jumps in and says that is not a proper thing to say.

"Porcha will tell Chad he needs some jungle fever, we all laugh and Joanne says 'Chad, you can tell Porcha that you find that offensive.' We all roll our eyes and Chad tells Joanne to chillax.

"Then Chad tells Dale, who is Vietnamese, that he must have learned how to drive in the rice paddies. We all laugh, but Joanne grabs Dale's arm and apologizes for us. Really? Dale calls Chad 'the Rabbi' all the time cuz he is Jewish, and Dale calls me the Pope cuz I am Catholic.

"Joanne jumps in and says she is worried that we should not be referring to each other in this way. The topper is I start to tell a joke about the two soldiers having sex with a dead alligator on a bus, and she jumps in and says that type of humor is just not funny. Can you believe that?"

Walker finishes the interview, types up his notes and obtains Angie's signature to make sure there are no additions or corrections. He interviews the remaining team members who share essentially the same views that she is tolerable at work, but they have no interest in being with her socially.

DOCUMENT: Walker types up all the memos from the meetings to document the interviews. He also reviews his personal reflections he had written after each interview. He arranges a meeting with Peggy (the supervisor) to determine the next steps. He will take copious notes of that meeting as well.

Peggy and Walker review the information that has been gathered. Peggy is concerned about the nature of the repartee between the team members and believes additional investigation is required. She asks Walker to revisit each team member to ask if any of them have been upset by any of the comments made focusing on their national origin, gender, religion, color, or race.

The supplemental interviews reveal that each member has no concerns with their bantering with each other even when it involves kidding about their being part of a protected group. They each say that this "messing with each other" is part of the team's camaraderie and bonding.

EVALUATE: There is little dispute as to the facts. Joanne is a good worker and does her job very well as do the other members of the team. It is clear that the employees do not want to socialize in any manner with Joanne outside of work. They find her actions vastly limit their enjoyment. A secondary issue that has surfaced indicates that the members of the team kid each other with slams and quips that may be inappropriate in a work setting, but all of the comments are outside of work.

Based on the investigation, the company determines that the failure to include Joanne has nothing to do with her inclusion in any protected category but simply that the other workers do not want to socialize with her outside of work.

RESPONSE: The supervisor, Peggy, and Walker develop potential responses to consider below:

- Move Joanne to a new team;
- Ask Dale and the team to include Joanne in lunches but not after work gatherings;
- Do nothing;
- Break up the team.

What are some other possible responses to consider? A key to good decision-making is being able to look at more than the obvious alternatives. Sometimes the best solution is one that does not present itself initially, but after investigating the matter thoroughly, a creative option may turn out to be the optimal response.

What about the comments the team members are making with their coworkers outside of work? Is that a problem for the company that might lead to someone claiming a hostile work environment? How should this be handled?

Management has been put on notice that the culture within this team embraces jokes based on protected class status. If a future complaint is made by an employee about this topic, there is a record that management was aware of the culture, and its response will be relevant.

Should management consider sensitivity training for all involved parties? What problems, issues, and potential responses should be examined in regard to the issue of the humor used outside of work being inappropriate, offensive, and unwelcome at work? Is a line being crossed that the employer must intervene, or is the company unnecessarily worried about being politically correct? Further, what if a customer or client of the company overhears a lunch hour conversation and takes offense? Should the company be concerned and should this behavior be addressed and curtailed?

You, as the person ultimately in charge of handling employee complaints as part of the CIDER method, must address these issues and document the evaluation and response.

Darlene has worked for the company for 6 years. She had her annual review performed by her supervisor, Rochelle this morning. Darlene was not happy with the meeting and went to the office manager, Yuji, to ask who she should see to file a complaint. Yuji accessed the office manual on his computer and pointed to the section on employee grievances.

"The manual says you are supposed to go see Rochelle to file a complaint."

"But my complaint is kinda about Rochelle, so that would be weird right?"

Yuji reads the company policy, "If Rochelle is out of the office, or an employee is uncomfortable bringing the grievance to Rochelle for any reason, the back-up person for this process is Jeffrey Robins."

"Thanks for the help."

"Ya know you could've looked this up on your own computer," Yuji yells, as Darlene smiles.

Darlene walks into Jeffrey's office ready to unload her frustrations. "Hi, I was told I am supposed to see you about registering a formal complaint."

"Well actually Rochelle is the staff member to see . . . unless she is out sick or on vacation."

"No, Rochelle is very much here, but the complaint is sort of about her, or at least I would feel weird spilling my guts to her, about her."

"Okay, I am your person. Give me a sec to get organized."

COMMUNICATE: Jeffrey shuts the door, gets out his paper, and places his iPad on the desk to use as a recorder. "I am going to take notes of what we discuss, but I don't want to miss anything so I want to record the meeting to make sure no important point is missed." Jeffrey starts recording. "Darlene, are you aware I am recording this?"

"Yes."

"Do I have your full permission and consent for recording this meeting?"

"Of course."

**Some employers record employees secretly leading to serious concerns. An employer should be up front with employees about being audio or video recorded. The company will have them acknowledge the recording and give their consent. The key to avoiding issues is the employee's expectation of privacy. When recording employees in the regular course of business, there should be documentation that the company advised the employees that they are being monitored. The recordings should also be used to compliment and reward employee actions instead of only using them punitively.

Jeffrey picks up his pen and pad and says, "You probably know this, but I am Jeffrey Robins. I am one of the representatives designated by the company to handle employee concerns. As our office manual says, we take every employee grievance seriously and investigate all filed complaints. My job today is to make sure we hear and understand all your concerns. The present goal is to perform a complete interview to learn everything that is on your mind so we can fully investigate the matter. Okay, the best way to start is for you to help me understand your frustration."

"I just had my annual performance meeting and it seemed really unfair. For the last 5 years I have gotten my review and a nice raise. Today Rochelle says my work is decent, but I have missed far too many days and she is going to leave my salary right where it is. She says she never knows if I will be at work. I mean, c'mon. I have missed some time, but I always call in to let the company know I won't be in. It is not like I just don't show up."

"Did Rochelle give you any other feedback?"

"Yeah, she gave me a written warning saying if I miss more than 10 days in the next 6 months, I will be subject to discipline up to and including termination."

Darlene hands the memorandum to Jeffrey.

"May I make a copy of this for my report at the end of our meeting?" Darlene nods.

Jeffrey continues making sure he is facilitating Darlene's willingness to outline all the details, using body language to convey interest.

"Had you received any prior warnings about absences?"

"No written ones, but Rochelle has been calling me 'Miss A. Lot' instead of Darlene. I will admit I have missed a lot of time in the last 4 months, but it is not like I am heading to the golf course. I have had some serious personal stuff that I had to tend to. My mom has cancer and since my dad died last year, I have had to take care of her when things get really bad."

"Oh, I am sorry about your mom." (While it has been emphasized repeatedly not to react to what the interviewee says, in this case it would be robot-like to ignore the revelation of Darlene's seriously ill mom. In addition, Jeffrey's comment does not give any indication of an evaluation.)

"Well, at some point it will end, but I am gonna miss more time periodically in the next year."

"I want to make sure I understand. Is it your complaint that you should have received a raise, or that you should not have received a warning, or that Rochelle was treating you unfairly?"

"You know maybe some of each. I mean I guess I did not expect a big raise, but the warning and that I may lose my job seems unfair after all my good years with this company."

The meeting goes on for 15 more minutes. Jeffrey copies the memo and types up the summary along with writing out his personal impressions. He marks his flash drive that has the recording of the interview for filing with his notes and schedules a meeting with the CIDER supervisor, Talia, to review the complaint.

INVESTIGATE: Jeffrey meets with Talia to outline the next steps of the investigation. Jeffrey summarizes Darlene's complaint to Talia and provides her with a copy of the executed statement. Talia asks him what he thinks are the next steps.

Jeffrey says, "I think this complaint falls under the umbrella of an employee not being happy with her raise, and that really does not need to be investigated further. I mean we can talk to Rochelle, but it is just the way it works. The supervisor has full authority to make appraisal and salary decisions."

Talia scans the statement of Darlene and asks, "Are there are any red flags jumping out at you from your interview?"

"It seems pretty straightforward to me. I mean Darlene admits she has missed a great deal of work. I pulled her absence record and it is pretty serious. She is an At-Will employee. The way I see it, she is plenty lucky she was not fired already for missing so much time. I would file this under, 'Too bad, so sad' and that would be end of the investigation."

Talia smiles, takes out a booklet, and hands it to Jeffrey. "I think you need to read this information on the FMLA in-depth and let's meet again in two hours."

The Family Medical Leave Act (FMLA) of 1993 (2006) is known to some as the law about maternity leave, and while it does contain a section on maternity time off, the Act was designed to provide job security and appropriate leave periods for employees with personal or family related, serious health issues. (Family and Medical Leave Act of 1993 29 U.S.C. §§ 2602–2654 [2006]).

Companies are not obligated to provide the FMLA leave unless the company has 50 or more employees in 20 or more workweeks in the current or preceding calendar year. However, all public agencies and all public or private elementary or secondary schools, regardless of the number of employees it employs, must provide FMLA benefits.

The FMLA entitles eligible employees to take unpaid, job-protected leave for specified family and medical reasons with continuation of group health insurance coverage under the same terms and conditions as if the employee had not taken leave.

To be eligible an employee must have worked for the company for at least 1 year and had to log at least 1,250 hours of work at the company in the year immediately preceding the requested leave.

The employee's job with the company is to be protected during the leave. If the employee takes the FMLA leave as a supervisor, and when they come back the company has demoted them to errand person, this is an employer violation.

Eligible employees are entitled to 12 weeks (does not need to be consecutive) of leave in a 12-month period for: the birth of a child, adoption, approved foster care, care for the employee's spouse, child, or parent who has a serious health condition, or if the employee has a serious health condition that prevents him or her from working.

A dispute often revolves around the definition of "serious health condition." To prove the health condition is serious, the employee must demonstrate that the condition in question requires continued treatment by a health care provider and includes a period of incapacity of more than 3 days or is a chronic health condition under the care of a physician (such as diabetes). Employers have the right to request medical certification of the condition. Treating the employee with respect and listening to their concerns will reduce the number of lawsuits in this and all areas of employment law.

An employer's attempt to assert that the employee in question never told them why they were missing time from work will rarely be a successful defense to a claim that the worker's FMLA rights were being ignored. The onus is on the employer to make sure employees are aware of their rights.

Jeffrey returns later in the day to meet with Talia and review the complaint after acquainting himself with the FMLA.

"Whoa, we may have really screwed up if Darlene's supervisor based her salary review and warning on her missing work because she had to take care of her mom who has cancer, which would be clearly classified as a serious health condition. I have a couple of questions.

"Does our company have more than 50 employees since I see if we don't, we are not under a legal obligation to follow the FMLA? The other question is why didn't you just tell me about the FMLA stuff right away?"

"Well to answer the second question, I am a teacher first and I had to learn this stuff, and it sticks far better this way than if I just tell you. In regard to our company being bound by the FMLA, no, we have only 30 qualified employees."

"Okay, now I am confused again. You point out that Darlene's absences fall under the FMLA, but it turns out that our company does not have to worry about that."

"Right now, we don't, but we are a growing company, and at some point, we will hit that magic number requiring us to provide FMLA benefits, and we need to monitor that. When the time comes, we will need to educate the staff on their rights."

"How should we respond to Darlene?"

"While you were brushing up on the FMLA specifics, I met with Rochelle to investigate Darlene's concerns." Talia reaches for her notes and goes on.

"There seems to be no factual issues in dispute. Rochelle says Darlene had been a great employee for years. The big problem is not her work product, but the fact that she has missed 39 days in the last 6 months and that has put a huge burden on other employees in her department.

"Rochelle is aware that Darlene's mom has cancer and feels bad, but says missing so much work is a real problem. In regard to the warning, Rochelle felt she owed it to Darlene to be direct and to let her know the seriousness of her absences. Oh, and when I asked if she ever called Darlene "Miss A. Lot," she said that she was trying to be funny."

DOCUMENT: The recorded statements of Darlene and Rochelle were marked and matched with the typed versions along with a written analysis of the FMLA requirements. Furthermore, written confirmation from the business office that the company did not have 50 or more employees at any point in the last year and thus is not required to provide employees with FMLA benefits was obtained. A record of Darlene's absences was placed with the investigation materials along with a detailed written summary of the meetings between Talia and Jeffrey.

EVALUATION: Jeffrey and Talia discuss the issues and the material compiled to date to determine if any additional investigation should be pursued. Talia opines no further interviews need to be conducted since there is no factual dispute. Talia also obtains Darlene's salary history with the company.

Jeffrey: "I am really baffled. If I understand this correctly, if we had more employees so that the FMLA rules applied to us, the actions of the company would be potentially illegal. I mean, although she is not being fired right now, her qualifying FMLA missed time from work is being used against her, and we did not advise her regarding her rights. Yet because the company does not have the 50 employees, we don't have to worry about any of this. Am I seeing this situation correctly?"

Talia: "You are on the right path. I need to meet with the CEO to determine how he wants to handle these issues not just from the company's legal standpoint, but also from the ethical perspective. But one thing is certain, it is imperative this company immediately institute a policy to record details of employee absences."

RESPONSE: What are the options for a proper response to Darlene's complaint and what are your recommendations?

In addition, if this was your company and you had less than 50 employees (not under the FMLA jurisdiction) how would you address these issues of workers missing vast amounts of time for serious health conditions or if they had family members with serious health conditions?

In the same vein (the company is not required to provide FMLA benefits since they have less than 50 employees) how would you handle maternity leave differently than time off for serious health conditions? Giving employees up to 12 weeks off and paying benefits may be a hardship on the business with so few employees (considering cost and pressure on other employees) so what is the policy you would have in place? What are some alternatives? If you decide you will give 6 weeks maternity leave, but only to the pregnant woman and not the father, is that gender discrimination?

Remember, it is important that whatever policy is instituted, it be administered to all employees fairly and does not treat any members of a protected category differently than other employees.

The company needs to implement a system requiring that whenever employees miss more than a few days of work that the employee completes, dates, and signs a form outlining the specific reason(s) for the absences. If the company meets the FMLA threshold, the form must include language from the employer explaining the employee's right to FMLA benefits.

FOLLOW-UP: The company needs to carefully monitor the situation as it approaches the magic number of employees (50), which will make the FMLA guidelines mandatory. Training and education will need to be instituted immediately upon reaching that number of employees.

Five More Employment Complaint Scenarios for Analysis

This chapter outlines five separate employee complaints to examine and uses the CIDER method to properly investigate, evaluate, and respond. The difference between these examples and the past three examples in Chapters Eighteen to Twenty is that the reader will be working without a net. As the information unfolds in each scenario, less guidance is provided; consequently, the reader must step up the brain activity and more actively utilize the CIDER method to handle the process to completion.

True learning takes place when a person is able to use information gained from past experiences and successfully apply those lessons and knowledge to new situations. The employee grievances are presented, but the last several steps of the CIDER process, especially the evaluation and response, are in your hands.

Scenario 1: National Origin

Anaya has worked for the company for over 2 years. She has a bindi on her forehead. A bindi is a nonpermanent mark centered generally on the lower forehead between the eyebrows. The mark is worn by women of Hindu or Jain faith. There are different colors worn for different occasions. This woman is wearing a red mark

© Abir Bhattacharya/Shutterstock.com

to signify that she is married. It also represents true love and prosperity.

Anaya comes to your office to meet with you, the individual identified for office personnel to register complaints. You ask her to sit down and close the door.

She says she hates to be a bother, but she is very frustrated with some of the other employees. Anaya explains that approximately 2 months ago Robbie called her "Dot" while pointing at her forehead. She tried to laugh it off the first time, but he continued to call her that name several times a day. And now the name has caught on and others in the company call her Dot.

"Now Gary, Zoe, Rhea and Loren call me Dot. I just wish it would stop, but I worry if I tell them to stop, they will think I am . . . well one of those people. I don't want to get shunned or ignored by my coworkers." The meeting with Anaya goes for another 10 minutes until you are convinced she has told you all of her concerns.

For the first step of the investigation you meet with Robbie in your office. You articulate the preamble that explains the company's policy in regard to investigating complaints.

Robbie admits to calling Anaya "Dot" and does not disagree or dispute Anaya's timeline or details. Robbie believes the name is funny and says Anaya knows he is just messing with her. Robbie says, "The nickname is just Dot, and that is not offensive. It is not like I am calling her some horrible name like . . . well you know what I mean and besides, Dot is a really cute nickname and fits her perfectly."

Each of the four other employees during their respective interviews said Robbie told them Anaya likes being called Dot. Gary, Zoe, Rhea, and Loren all state they call her that name and that Anaya never complained or seemed bothered by that moniker.

The CIDER method must be employed. Go through the necessary steps and outline the red flag issues. What other aspects should be investigated? What is your evaluation? What are the possible responses, and which is best? What would you be concerned with regarding the follow-up?

Scenario 2: Looks Count

You are the primary employee to hear all employee grievances and complaints. Recently the position of receptionist opened up in your company. Sheila has been working for your employer for over 3 years in the file room. She has been a valued employee based on her work. She applied for the receptionist position. She was told she was one of two finalists for the position. The human resource department set up an interview with Paul Gottfried, who would make the final hiring decision.

Sheila comes to your office crying and saying she just met with Mr. Gottfried, who told her he is hiring the other candidate as the receptionist for the company. She relays to you that he told her that the receptionist is the first representative people see when coming to the office, and he is not comfortable with her in that role.

Sheila said, "I pressed Mr. Gottfried for his reasoning. He said he would rather not say. I said I am a big girl and can take whatever his concerns are. I tell him I want to know my weaknesses so I can improve. So, he takes a deep breath and says my weight is a detriment to the company image.

"I know I am about 25 lb higher than what is considered average, but I dress neatly, I am not sloppy, but well . . . he made me feel like I am a gross pig. This seems really unfair. I know I'm not Ms. Perfect Body, but that shouldn't matter."

The meeting continues for another 15 minutes. After Sheila leaves you contact the human resource director who informs you that Sheila outperformed the other candidate on the tests that are given to all applicants. Furthermore, she was recommended since she was an in-house candidate, while the other finalist did not presently work for the company. The company prefers to promote from within.

This scenario requires some research on the employment law. As discussed it is imperative a company should identify the protected categories in regard to all complaints to flush out the potential claims and allegations that may be alleged. The situation provides another difficult area for companies. Weight is not a protected category. The case of Cook v. Rhode Island Department of Mental Retardation is confusing since some read the decision and believe the court has made weight a protected category, but that is not correct (Cook v. Rhode Island Department of Mental Retardation 10 F.3d 17 [1993]).

The court of appeals decision stated that when a person's morbid obesity (Ms. Cook was 5'2" 320 lb) is so significant as to rise to the level of the ADA definition of disability, then the person is in a protected class based on disability status, not weight. Consequently, if an applicant is 20 lb overweight, they are not disabled. The individual's weight is not protected until he or she meets the criteria of the ADA definition (a physical or mental impairment that substantially limits a major life activity).

The point is that Sheila is not in a protected category (except in the state of Michigan, the only state in our country recognizing weight as a protected category). If the investigation reveals that the company did discriminate based on Sheila's weight, they are not violating the law.

The fact that weight is not a protected category is emphasized by a New Jersey appeals court's ruling. In that case, a casino had an appearance clause stating that waitstaff had to keep their weight within 7% of their hiring weight. The court found that clause was not illegal discrimination. The court went on to clarify that to have a viable lawsuit, an employee fired for a weight gain must prove a documented medical condition or post-pregnancy condition to pursue claims of gender discrimination. If the weight gain can be shown to be a result of pregnancy, then the case is changed from weight to gender discrimination. (Schiavo, et al. v. Marina District Dev. Co., LLC d/b/a Borgata Casino Hotel & Spa, No. A-5983-12 [(N.J. App. Div. Sept. 17, 2015]).

The key is always looking to see if any protected categories are involved. If the company only considers weight for female employees and not male workers, that may give rise to a viable claim of illegal discrimination since the employer is differentiating by a worker's inclusion in a protected category.

The casino justified their actions by stating it is good business to demand "reasonable workplace appearance, grooming and dress standards." The casino also stated that their weight clause was necessary because the company provided uniforms for waitstaff and did not want to constantly have to pay for new outfits.

Armed with this information, how should Sheila's complaint be handled? Yes, the quick answer is by using the CIDER method, but you must go through each element and expand on the questions and issues that should be addressed. What else do you want to know? What is your evaluation and response(s)?

Scenario 3: A Clever Employee's Trick

An interesting issue arises when an employee understands just enough about employment law to try to manipulate the system. In this scenario, the company has determined that they wish to discharge an employee, Molly, after giving her several written warnings over the course of the last 6 months about the low quality of her work.

The office manager, Alisha, asks Molly to come to her office and to bring her copy of the company manual. Molly is no dummy and is acutely aware that when she is asked to come with office manual in hand, it is not a good sign for continued employment.

When Molly walks in to the manager's office, she quickly surveys the room and sees Jimmy, the human resource director sitting in a chair with pen and paper in hand. Molly is aware that standard procedure when a company is planning to fire an employee is to have a second management team member present to be a witness to the process.

Alisha asks Molly to sit down. Alisha takes a deep breath, glances at Jimmy, and is just about to tell Molly she is being terminated when Molly jumps in.

"I am really glad you asked me to come here today. I wanted to tell you something, and I have been trying to figure out the best way to bring this horrible thing to the attention of the company. I will just come out and say it. I am being sexually harassed by Alan Thompson. He is always making jokes about my anatomy and letting me know that going to bed with him would be a life affirming experience."

If Alisha's next words to Molly were what she had planned on saying, "You're fired," Molly would claim the company was retaliating against her for filing a sexual harassment claim and likely commence a lawsuit against the company for wrongful termination.

Molly's knowledge of the law gave her the idea to turn herself into a whistle blower to try to protect her job. If a jury heard that as soon as the employee reported that she was being sexually harassed, the manager fired her on the spot, it would likely reach a verdict against the employer.

What should be done? What should not be done is follow through with the firing within moments of Molly informing the company of the claim of sexual harassment. A complaint has been filed by an employee. The CIDER method must be utilized immediately.

If Molly were terminated as planned, the investigation could not proceed in the orderly manner required. Alisha must immediately refer Molly to the company's representative designated to hear all employee grievances.

The company must begin the systematic investigation that is mandatory for each and every complaint as set forth by the CIDER method. The fact that the company was about to discharge the person who is filing the report is not relevant to the initial phase of the investigation. In fact, there is no reason to make the intake person to the complaint aware of the company's planned termination of Molly.

COMMUNICATE: Carson is the company's representative designated to meet with workers who wish to make the company aware of any concerns, complaints, or grievances. Molly must immediately be referred to Carson to report her complaint and initiate the process.

The complaint will be handled using the CIDER method. When the process reaches the evaluation stage, the timing of Molly's complaint should be part of the assessment of credibility. If it turns out Molly's sexual harassment complaint against Alan Thompson was without merit, should the company follow through with her termination?

The company must not ignore the obvious that Molly is likely litigious and will sue. Consequently, the company better have solid documentation of her poor work performance to rebut the timing of the termination and her allegation that she was fired solely for filing the sexual harassment complaint.

In the event the company finds that Molly's sexual harassment claim has merit, they will need to decide the best response to not only the inappropriate behavior of Alan Thompson, but also what to do with regard to Molly's status.

This scenario requires a cost-benefit analysis along with the other factors when evaluating the proper response. There is little doubt that if the company terminates Molly, she will, at a minimum, file an EEOC complaint and likely will bring a civil lawsuit for wrongful termination based on sexual harassment, retaliation, and whistleblower status.

To defend this lawsuit the company must prove the dismissal was unrelated to Molly filing her complaint, but was based on her poor performance. Furthermore, when she also alleges the poisoned work environment of sexual harassment, and how she tried to tolerate this horrible situation until she was let go, how will those allegations play out? Outline all possible options to respond based on the findings that her sexual harassment claims are justified, and the options if the company found her allegations against Alan Thompson are unfounded.

Scenario Four: A Nonemployee

Doug is a receptionist at Acme Financial. Hundreds of clients come through the door each day. Doug's duties include answering client questions and directing them to the proper offices for their meetings. The company has 75 employees in the building.

In the last several months Ruby, a client of Acme with a large portfolio, has been in her words "flirting" with Doug at a very intense level. She has been whispering in his ear, texting naked pictures of herself and today put a key in his hand and said she would be waiting for him at 9:00 pm tonight in the hotel room.

Doug went to his boss, Phillip, to complain about the problem. Phillip said, "Yeah, I have seen Ruby flirt with you. She seems to be really into you."

"I don't want her being into me. It makes me really uncomfortable, and I need it to stop. I asked her to please keep the comments professional, but she just says that she was always told no means yes."

Phillip says, "You know she doesn't work here so I can't do much to stop it, plus she brings in about a hundred grand a year for the company. I wish I could do more, but I think you should just smile and make her feel like a valued client."

"But I really am uncomfortable whenever she walks in."

"Look, she is a really important client and as long as she doesn't touch you, it is fine. Remember . . . the customer is always right."

How should this be handled? Does it matter that Ruby is not an employee? What are the options for the company's response?

Scenario Five: The British Are Coming

An employee, Holly, goes in the bathroom and puts on her underwear on the outside of her pants and runs through the office yelling, "The British are coming; the British are coming." Virtually everyone in the office thinks it is hysterical except Jennifer. Is that a problem, or does Jennifer need to relax?

While the majority of the office staff seem to find Holly's actions hysterical and a day brightener, Jennifer immediately goes to the office of the company's designated representative to file a complaint.

Jennifer reports that she is embarrassed by Holly's actions. She says, "Everyone was watching my reaction because they think I'm the office prude. I don't need to come to a job and have people running around in their underwear. It is not professional, it is crude and gross. Can't I just come to work and not worry that I may have to see actions that make me feel embarrassed? I know some thought it was fun, and everyone loves Holly, but this is over the top and not funny to me."

How should this be handled? Who should be interviewed? What are viable alternatives? Does it matter that Holly has been working at the company for over 10 years and is a great employee and Jennifer has been with the company for under a year?

What are the key differences and similarities between this scenario and the Chapter Nineteen scenario titled, "They won't ask me to join them for lunch?" To get this started, one issue is behavior at work as opposed to conduct outside of work.

The Fun Never Stops: Five Additional Scenarios to Hone the CIDER Skills

The next five potential work situations (scenarios 6–10) give more opportunities to get comfortable with examining problems on a more in-depth basis. If you are reading these various situations, and your reaction is to shrug your shoulders and say, "Just tell these people to lighten up," there may be a problem.

It is essential that any serious look at the scenarios should stir up numerous questions and concerns. A person does not need to have all the answers but must recognize the potential issues, understand what questions to ask, and know where to find the answers.

The importance of obtaining all the relevant information to properly evaluate the case and respond to the behavior should now be ingrained. Furthermore, a working knowledge of employment law instills the ability to properly analyze the potential issues. Understanding the concepts set forth in this text enables each of you to handle employee complaints in a manner that does not simply scratch the surface, but is thorough in hitting all the elements of the CIDER method.

Communicate, Investigate, Document, Evaluate, and Respond is not just something to memorize for an exam, it is the best way to ensure less litigation and improve the workplace atmosphere for all employees.

Scenario Six: But I'm Okay With It

Barb is the supervisor for the warehouse and is responsible for 25 employees who work on the dock. Her duties include scheduling, discipline, and evaluations. Barb is confined to a wheelchair as a result of a disability.

Erik, the receptionist who does not work on the loading dock, comes in to file a complaint. He was delivering a document to Barb when a warehouse worker came in to Barb's office to request a day off.

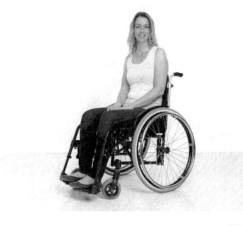

© Firma V/Shutterstock.com

Erik says, "So I'm talking to Barb and this guy walks in and says, 'Hey Wheels, you got a second?' I mean I am floored. Calling her Wheels? Really?! This guy is not only being disrespectful to his boss, but is making fun of her for being in a wheelchair. I guess I am not the type of person who thinks making fun of the handicapped is funny."

You, the interviewer, meet with Barb to continue the investigation. You articulate the standard preamble emphasizing that all complaints are investigated without exception.

"Barb, it has been brought to our attention that an employee is calling you Wheels."

"Oh, most of the people in the loading dock call me Wheels as homage to my wheelchair. I assume Erik complained because when he heard Rocky call me Wheels, he just about fainted. I want you to know that not only do I not mind being called Wheels, I like it. It shows the employees are not tiptoeing around me and aren't pitying me. I would hate it if someone told them to stop using that nickname, or if they became self-conscious about kidding me."

How should this be handled with regard to the investigation, evaluation, and response?

Scenario Seven: She Is Dropping "F" Bombs

The senior vice-president, Candace, usually keeps her office door open. When she is on the phone with clients and friends, her language is filled with expletives. Her administrative assistant, Richard, has come to you to file a complaint.

COMMUNICATE: You ask Richard to sit down; you take your pad and pen and ask him to tell you what is on his mind.

Richard begins, "I feel a little scared coming in because . . . well I

© svershinsky/Shutterstock.com

have a complaint about my boss, and I am worried I will get in trouble."

You must reassure the employee that the company encourages employees to make the company aware of all their concerns. It is important to emphasize that the company does not allow any retaliatory conduct toward employees who come forward with complaints.

Richard continues, "Ya know Candace? Well, when she gets angry or excited, the expletives fly. I told her the words really bother me. She said I needed to grow a pair and graduate from nursery school. I have tried tuning the words out, but each swear word really upsets me. I once closed her door, and she yelled at me, saying she gets claustrophobic and to never do that again."

How would the CIDER method proceed? What would you want to learn about the situation that is not apparent to evaluate this properly and respond accordingly? What are some red flags? Outline the potential responses.

It is important that the specific language is determined since some language may be sexual in nature or racially offensive and may give rise to a hostile work environment. The case of Reeves v. C.H. Robinson Worldwide, Inc. illustrated that offensive language need not be targeted at the plaintiff in order to support a Title VII hostile work environment claim. The language must be severe and pervasive (Reeves v. C.H. Robinson Worldwide, Inc. 525 F.3d 1139 [11th Cir. 2008]).

Earlier in this book the concept of a hostile work environment was outlined. Do not revert back to thinking, "Hey, swearing is hostile and it is work, so hence a hostile work environment." When looking at potential liability, the status of discrimination based on protected categories must be at the forefront of the analysis.

Scenario Eight: But He Hugged Her First

Communicate—Julie walks in to your office and says, "I am so upset and creeped out. Sharon came up to me and put her arms around me and told me I looked like I needed a major league hug. You know Sharon is gay, and her actions really invaded my personal space. Sharon was being very sexual."

"Have you had any other encounters with her that made you feel uncomfortable?"

"No, but this was so intense, and I haven't been able to get this off my mind."

"Did you say anything to her?"

"I was too stunned."

The meeting goes on for another 10 minutes until Julie says she has nothing else to add to the encounter. You take down all the information. Your next step is to meet with the CIDER supervisor to plan the remainder of the investigation.

The supervisor and you agree that the first step is to interview Sharon and once that is completed to schedule another meeting to determine what direction the rest of the investigation should take.

Sharon comes to your office. You go through the usual statement advising her that the company investigates all complaints without exception.

"Julie brought a concern to the attention of the company that you hugged her, and this made her very uncomfortable. Do you recall this incident?"

Sharon gets very stiff in her chair and says, "Yes, I knew her dog died the day before, and I saw Billy hug her, and she told him how she needed that. I noted how happy it made her when Billy hugged her, so when I saw her later that morning I gave her a hug since I knew she liked it."

The conversation goes on for 15 minutes. An interview summary is typed for Sharon's signature confirming the accuracy of the entire conversation.

The investigation continues with you interviewing Billy, who comes to the office and sits down. After going through the standard opening before starting the interview you begin.

"Sharon said she saw you and Julie hug; do you have a recollection of that incident?"

"Why does Sharon care if I am hugging Julie? Julie and I have been friends for the last 7 years. Her husband and I are golfing buddies, my wife and Julie do Yoga together and the four of us travel often. So now why is this any of Sharon's business?"

"We are investigating a concern and are just trying to compile relevant information."

How should this be handled? Who else should be interviewed? Should the company prohibit hugging? What would be the teaching and training to help employees understand the issues better?

Scenario Nine: Taco Tuesday

A bulletin board at the company serves many purposes allowing employees to post birthday messages, coupons for restaurants, cute cartoons, and other forms of communication. One morning someone posts a coupon and ad for "Taco Tuesday" at a local restaurant.

The next Tuesday someone puts a flyer that they made up to look like the Taco Tuesday ad, but instead it says "Tantalizing Tuesday" to let employees know to meet at a local bar after work. The next Tuesday another flyer is posted for "Touch Me Tuesday" inviting staff to a happy hour. The next week another note goes up in the same type style as the other notices that reads, "Tongue Me Tuesday" inviting staff to an ice-cream parlor.

No complaints have been filed by any employees. Should the company put a stop to these bulletin board posts or allow them to continue until there is a complaint?

TACO TUESDAY

ALL YOU CAN EAT TACOS

There is an additional issue to consider when evaluating this and other similar situations; when an employer knowingly allows something to continue, the employer is complicit. One business had a bulletin board that employees used to post jokes, articles, and quips to share with the staff. Some of the postings were on the edge of appropriate with overt sexuality. The owner decided he would ignore the questionable material, but if there were ever a complaint, he would immediately take down the bulletin board.

One day an employee did not like that a photograph of her head was pasted on the body of a swimsuit model and tacked up on the bulletin board. She was livid and filed a grievance. The owner, after hearing of the complaint, called a staff meeting and announced that effective immediately the board was being taken down for good.

Subsequent to the meeting, several workers came in to complain that it was not fair and everyone loved the sharing of humor. The owner said he would not allow any employee to feel uncomfortable and that was the end of the discussion.

A company must consider that an employee could reasonably assert that the owner was keenly aware of the presence of the objectionable material on the board and, by allowing it to remain, permitted a sexually charged culture to exist. Further, the worker may successfully claim it was useless to file a complaint when the owner already had knowledge of the situation yet did not remedy or even address the problem.

How should the matter of the bulletin board and the weekly flyers with various takes on Taco Tuesday be handled? Should the company wait for a complaint to come before acting?

Scenario Ten: But It Is Funny

Mike is an extroverted employee, which is probably why he is the top salesperson in the company. He works mostly outside the office calling on clients but comes in at least a few hours a week to drop off items and to attend meetings. When he walks in the building, he holds court with many of the staff telling them stories and jokes. His presence at the workplace is obvious because of the crowds and laughter with Mike in the center of it all.

Mike made his appearance at the office in the morning. As soon as he walks out the door to chants of "Mikey-Mikey," Roger is in your office.

You are the representative who the company has hired and trained to handle all employee complaints. The supervisor of the CIDER method is out of the office for the next 3 weeks and has told you to handle any complaints from start to finish in his absence. He emphasized if you are not confident in some aspect of the investigation during his absence, you should con-tact the attorney the company uses for employment questions.

COMMUNICATE: Roger is a fre-quent visitor to your office since he tends to make a complaint about ev-ery 2 months about something, from someone re-programming his phone to coworkers stealing his stash of M&M's. Roger knows the drill, and he even closes the door as he walks in.

"So, Mike graced us with his magical presence. He is so full of him-self. He was so politically incorrect today I had to register a complaint. He begins his monologue by choosing to tell everyone about how they can get free M&M's by waiting until I go to lunch and taking them from my desk in the top left-hand drawer.

"Okay, I know that is not so politically incorrect, but when he divulges the whereabouts of my M&M's, he points at me. The group all looked at me and laughed. Then he tells this joke that was so wrong and upsetting. It makes fun of Hispanics. I mean the joke hurt me, and I don't even like the Hispanic guy, Gio."

"Did you say anything?"

"Yes, I did. I told Mike that it is not funny to say hurtful things. He said, 'Are we still talking about the M&M's?' I say, 'No. I am talking about your joke.' He says, 'let's ask Gio if he thought it was funny.' Gio sells out his entire country and says it was very funny. Mike says if Gio is not bothered, then I should chill out and go to the store and get him more M&M's which again makes everyone look at me and laugh."

"Have you heard Mike tell other objectionable jokes?"

"Yes, I have, but today I decided to stop burying my head in the sand and expose his behavior."

You take very detailed notes and ask Roger to repeat the joke and any other inappropriate jokes he has heard Mike tell.

INVESTIGATE: You call Mike and ask him to come back to your office for a meeting. You begin to interview him in regard to Roger's complaint. You have a card that reminds you of the key phrases to use before questioning each person to assure Mike no judgments have been made and that the company investigates all complaints. You also have prepared questions to make sure you do not just wing it. Normally, you would have met with the supervisor to formulate questions together, but since he was gone, it forced you to analyze the issues on your own leading to an expansion of your skills.

"Mike, when you were here earlier today, do you remember telling a joke?"

"I told a bunch of jokes. It is my way."

Do you recall telling one that Roger expressed some concerns over and you asked Gio if he thought it was funny?"

"Oh, I definitely do. The M&M man objected. He thought in some way it was not a good joke, but trust me, the joke was funny and not just kinda funny, but fall on the floor funny."

"Would you mind telling me the joke?"

"Okay, but I want to start out by saying I don't mean to be racist, but . . ."

It should be common knowledge that when someone says "I don't mean to be racist but . . ." the next thing out of that person's mouth will be among the most racist thing you will ever hear. Mike's joke falls into that category. You want to say to him, "Are you kidding me with that stuff?" But you know this is the time to compile information only and not evaluate or render any editorial opinions since that will inhibit the remainder of the interview.

"Mike, do you tell this joke to our clients?"

"I sure do and lots of even better ones. It is part of why clients love me."

You continue the interview until you have obtained more depth on Mike's jokes as well as making sure he has told you anything relevant to his position. You type up the summary of the interview and obtain his signature verifying its accuracy.

You review Mike's confidential personnel file and see a complaint made by an employee 2 years ago against Mike for telling sexual jokes that made an employee feel uncomfortable. The evaluation and response are set forth in the file. Mike received a written warning to immediately stop telling any jokes or making any comments that are insensitive to any group. The warning went on to say this applies while at work or in the presence of any employees.

What further investigation should you pursue? What is your evaluation of the situation, and what are some options for a response? Is there one response that you believe is the best?

CIDER in Action

There are some complaints that appear to be just silly little office politics or cliquish behavior that seem unlikely to lead to a viable lawsuit or a hostile work environment claim. The problem is the company will not know the full extent of the issues until they have followed the CIDER method. The only way that occurs is by taking each complaint seriously no matter how frivolous it may appear initially. As noted in the CIDER process, the first phase of communicating does not involve evaluating the legitimacy or seriousness of the employee's complaint.

Even when there is a CIDER system in place, managers need to be trained that it is not their job to assess the validity of the complaint; rather, they need to refer the complaining employee to the appropriate person who will follow the CIDER protocol. A company does not want the CIDER method circumvented by a well-meaning supervisor.

It is likely that an astute person would have a sense that some of the employee concerns being raised are nitpicky and not worth company time to examine. But the problem is when that assumption is wrong, the company will have ignored an issue that was brought to their attention, allowing a situation to fester that should have been recognized and handled right away.

The company must err on the side of caution and investigate each complaint. Some classic actual employee complaints are:

- Someone is stealing my lunch/snack/drink
- Someone is taking my pens/stapler/sticky notes
- The boss always puts me down
- John is a mouth breather, and it is really annoying
- Suzanne picks on me
- Chris passes gas constantly
- Tom makes fun of the lunch I bring. Today when I started eating my liverwurst sandwich, he asked if I had a death wish
- Katie wears too much perfume
- Brock always smells like onions, and it is really distracting
- Thuy is always making kissy sounds into the phone when talking to her husband

- Ray always steals the sports page
- Joe leaves a big mess in the breakroom
- Steve always takes up two spaces in the parking lot
- Terri always asks me to pitch in for birthday presents for people I don't even know
- Quisha takes up too much time in the bathroom
- Justin talks too loudly

While most of those complaints are indeed silly, some may give rise to a serious hostile work environment claim. The concern that the supervisor is favoring one employee over another may be nothing more than liking a hard worker over a lazy staffer or it could be a huge issue.

Since the company investigates each complaint, a review of the personnel file belonging to the supervisor who is the subject of the complaint may show that this is the fourth similar favoritism complaint by a minority. If the employer did not have a systematic method in place, they would not be aware of the potential minefield of discrimination based on inclusion in a protected category.

The implicit promise of the company is to investigate each employee complaint using the CIDER method. That means there will be some "wah-wah" moments, but it is imperative to listen carefully every time an employee files a grievance and make sure by implementing the CIDER method that there are no underlying serious issues.

Investigating each complaint, regardless of how it may appear on its face, takes the onus off any employee who would try to determine if the particular grievance deserves to go on to the next phase. The process is refined; when a complaint is made, the CIDER method is initiated. No exceptions.

The goal is not to make a workplace sterile and take away enjoyment and fun bantering among employees but to make sure when behavior rises to unwelcome and inappropriate levels, it is recognized and corrected.

The Changing Laws

The law and rules in the area of employment law are subject to change. A key is to keep up with the law and not just to know the current state of the law but to be aware of the environment. The best method for keeping up to date is to read current decisions in employment law cases regularly from the Federal Court of Appeals, U. S. Supreme Court, State Appellate Court and State Supreme Court in the particular state where the business is located. In addition, review the EEOC rulings and published decisions in regard to employer duties and obligations.

There are publications that report all pertinent cases with comments to help a person understand the ramifications of the decision. The Employment Law Report, a monthly update for important legal developments, is an excellent source to stay on top of the employment issues. In addition, the Desktop Encyclopedia of Employment Law is another great resource for employment law. There are other online journals that will help a reader expand his or her knowledge in this area. Another wonderful source is the Great Lakes ADA Center. They write legal briefings on various issues that are extremely helpful. Brief 13 from June 2010 entitled "Invisible Disabilities and the ADA" is superb and a great source of valuable information (http://accessibilityonline.s3.amazonaws.com/archives/2010-06-02_Invisible_Disabilities_and_the_ADA_Brief_13.pdf).

A person can also just go on the Internet and enter recent employment law court cases into the browser and hit enter. Or the search can be refined to current judicial decisions for each protected category. Keeping up with the legal precedents is a great advantage to make sure a person sees the winds of change.

Employees will say inappropriate things, and that will get employers in trouble. The key is looking to see if the conduct is severe enough to affect the victim's working conditions and to make sure the investigation goes beyond skimming the surface to uncover if the victim is targeted because of his inclusion in a protected category.

Helping your business prevent large damage payments and liability for discrimination along with making the workplace the best it can be is the thrust of this book. Handling complaints properly and thoroughly utilizing the CIDER method will limit exposure to lawsuits.

Companies must apply all rules and policies consistently to avoid a claim that some employees are being treated differently based on protected status. Businesses must teach, train, and educate all the employees to recognize and address common pitfalls. Furthermore, companies must adopt policies emphasizing that inappropriate conduct will not be tolerated by the company.

The goal is not just to limit liability but to have a great atmosphere where employees can flourish and be proud of their working environment. Implementing the CIDER method into the core and fabric of the company's procedures will help recognize and alleviate serious misconduct and limit exposure to lawsuits.

Examples of Documenting the CIDER Method

The reader at this point in the book is clear on the method for handling each complaint. The last piece of the puzzle involves the types of documentation required to effectively use the CIDER method.

The documents below stem from a situation in which an employee, Amy Phafoofnik, meets with the designated company representative, Josh Peters, to file a complaint. Amy outlines her grievances against Les S. Moore.

The sample documents are on separate pages to help the reader understand the CIDER process and proper protocol. The first document is a summary of the intake interview with the complaining employee (Amy Phafoofnik). Each interview summary is detailed with quotes signed by the individual being interviewed. The date, time, and location of the interview is also included. That protocol is imperative to confirm that the employee acknowledges that the documents properly represent their sentiments.

The next item documents the meeting between the investigator, Josh Peters, and the supervisor, Betsy Flannigan, during which they plan the investigation.

The next document is a summary of the interview with the person named in the complaint, Les S. Moore. The next three samples are summaries of the interviews with the witnesses, Mary Johnson, Joe Smith, and Kim Robertson.

The final document is the Evaluation and Response report. That report outlines the specifics and reasons for the company's determination. The conclusion of the report sets forth the responses that the company considered and ultimately selected to remedy the problems raised in the complaint.

Interview of Amy Phafoofnik

Amy Phafoofnik brought a complaint to the attention of the company. She met with Josh Peters on February 15, 2019, to outline her concerns. Amy said her supervisor Les S. Moore had been making her feel more and more uncomfortable with his words and actions.

Over the last several months, Les continually asked her out. Amy said, "Les was just asking me to join him for lunch. I thought that was fine and normal, but while at these lunches his questions would always turn to very personal issues. He asked me if my sex life was good. He also told me that his sex life used to be great, but now it needs a kickstart."

Amy said that after a few lunches he told her that he would like to see her after work and have a business dinner. She kept making excuses that she was busy hoping he would stop. "I was not sure how to handle this, but I was getting the feeling he was looking for some romance or action."

Amy said, "He also was always trying to hug me. I did hug him the first couple of times because I did not know how to stop the hug without being offensive. Now I am prepared and usually able to keep my distance. But he is persistent like an octopus with his arms."

Amy said she thought she had this under control and did not need to report his behavior until a few days ago. She explained, "On February 5, Les asked me to come in to his office. I walked in and he closed the door. He immediately tried to grab me, but I sat down right away to dodge that hug. He then knelt next to me and put his hand on my shoulder. He said he has been thinking about me constantly. He began stroking my shoulder as he said that he can't stop thinking about me when he is lying in his bed."

Amy said she did not know whether to slap him, quit, request a transfer, or file a complaint. She talked with her friends, and they urged her to make the company aware of his actions.

Amy says she has tried to avoid Les since that day and even called in sick twice when she was trying to decide what to do. "I asked Kim Robertson for some advice on what I should do."

Amy said that in the last few days Les tells her that what she is wearing is so sexy and that if she is trying to entice him it is working. "He just stares at me and says I am the most sensual woman he has ever seen. Now I am so self-conscious of whatever I am wearing. I needed to come here today and get this off my chest."

Amy says all the other people here are very professional and Les is the only individual at work who is not being professional.

The interview began at 10:00 am on February 15, 2019 and ended at 11:05 am.

I have read the above summary and it is true, accurate and complete.

Dated: **02/15/2019**

Signature: _____*Amy Phafoofnik*_____

Amy Phafoofnik

Summary Prepared by Josh Peters

Summary of the Investigation Meeting in Regard to the Complaint of Amy Phafoofnik

A conference was held on February 16, 2019, with Betsy Flannigan and Josh Peters to discuss the complaint made by Amy Phafoofnik against Les S. Moore to outline the scope of the investigation.

It was determined that Les S. Moore must be interviewed within 24 hours. In addition, Josh Peters will interview Mary Johnson and Joe Smith who have offices near Les and Amy. In addition, Kim Robertson will also be interviewed since Amy mentioned discussing matters with her at various times.

Betsy said she will review the personnel files of Les and Amy to see if other similar issues have been previously reported. Betsy asked that all other interviews be completed by February 20th.

Betsy assigned the interviews of the four employees to Josh Peters. We set a date for the evaluation meeting for 10:00 am on February 22, 2019. Betsy asked that I have all statements completed and on her desk before noon on February 21st.

We outlined questions for Les, and Betsy asked that Josh specifically address the following:

-Allegations he has asked her out

-Allegations he tries to hug her

-The February 5th meeting in Les's office where he said he is thinking of her while in bed and inappropriately touched her shoulder.

-In regard to questioning Kim Robertson, she asked that Josh find out what Amy has told her in addition to what Kim has observed.

The meeting started at 1:15 pm and ended at 2:15 pm.

Summary Prepared by: _____*Josh Peters*_____   Dated: 02/16/2019

Interview of Les S. Moore

I (Josh Peters) asked Les to come to my office for a private meeting on February 17, 2019. I closed the door and told Les a grievance had been filed naming him and that it is the company policy to investigate all complaints. I emphasized that the company has not made any determination regarding the merits of the complaint, but is simply compiling all information to properly assess the issues raised.

I mentioned Amy's complaint in general terms and asked him specifically about asking her out. He responded, "Did she really complain? I think there is quite a bit going on here. I mean first of all I am her boss and I have asked her to lunch, a business lunch. If she wants to fantasize that I am asking her on a date when it is a business lunch that seems to be her problem not mine."

Les went on to say that he goes out with other members of his staff and that is just a good way to get work done.

Les said yes, he had asked her to go out after work, but again to discuss business. "It is not like I was asking her to a hotel room."

We turned our attention to the February 5th meeting in his office. I asked him directly about her allegation that he touched her shoulder and told her he thinks about her when he is lying in bed.

Les said, "This is absurd. I did ask her to come into my office so I could privately inform her that some of her outfits are not appropriate for work. I explained that the one she was wearing on that day kept falling down and exposing her shoulder. I did reach and pull the drooping material back up. And in regard to me saying I am thinking of her in bed, I told her that when I woke up this morning, I was thinking about how I had to talk to her about her attire."

Les said he has never told her she looked sensual, but may have said her clothing is way too sexual for work.

The subject of hugging was brought up. "I have hugged her, but she has hugged me, too. Everyone around here hugs each other. I mean if that is the new company policy of no hugging, that is fine with me just send me a damn memo."

He said maybe the company should consider transferring Amy if she is going to be reading in so much to his innocent requests for a business lunch or his critique to dress more professionally.

Les wanted to make sure that we were aware that he is tired of this new movement where we blindly believe women and discount anything a man says. He wanted to stress that he did nothing wrong.

The interview began at 11:00 am on February 17th and ended at 12:05 pm.

I have read the above summary and it is true, accurate, and complete.

Dated: *02/17/2019*   Signature: _____*Les S. Moore*_____

                                                                                    Les S. Moore

Summary Prepared by Josh Peters

Interview of Kim Robertson

This is a summary of the meeting with Kim Robertson of February 20, 2019. The interview took place in the office of Josh Peters between Kim Robertson and Josh Peters.

I commenced the meeting by outlining the company policy to investigate all complaints and that the fact that we are investigating the complaint does not in any way mean the company has made any determination as to the merits of the issues.

I asked Kim if she was aware of any issues Amy was having with Les S. Moore, her supervisor.

Kim stated: "I am completely and fully aware. I told her his actions are horrible and she should report him. I don't know why she waited this long."

I asked Kim if she has seen any of their interactions.

She said, "I have been watching them like a hawk for the last 3 months. I wanted to run into his office and slap his sorry face, but she wouldn't let me. I wanted to run in here and tell you, but she asked me to let her take care of it."

Kim said she has seen Les wait for Amy to hug her. She also said she has watched Amy get more and more upset at work until she hated coming in. Kim said, "I have heard him tell her she is the sexiest woman in the world and desirable is not a strong enough word for her."

She showed me a video from her phone of him hugging her.

Kim said that Joe Smith and Mary Johnson have seen similar incidents as well, but they are scared to tell anyone because they think management will just side with Les.

The meeting started at 1:00 pm on February 20th and ended at 1:35 pm.

I have read the above summary and it is true, accurate, and complete.

Dated: *02/20/2019*   Signature: *Kim Robertson*

                                                                                       Kim Robertson

Summary Prepared by Josh Peters

Interview of Joe Smith

This is the summary of the statement of Joe Smith from the meeting with Josh Peters of February 20, 2019. The interview took place in Josh Peter's office.

Joe's office is next to Les S. Moore's office. Joe stated that he is aware of the tension between Les and Amy (Phafoofnik). "At first I was sure they were having an affair because they would hug and then she would go in his office and the door would close. But then Kim (Robertson) told me that Amy was not enjoying their interactions and then I understood that it was clear that Les was pushing himself on a very uncomfortable Amy."

Joe explained that he has heard Les give Amy many compliments on her clothes and her body. "I thought it was a bit over the top, but I thought just because I would never say something like that to a woman I worked with, I figured maybe I am outdated."

"I have heard Les often ask her to lunch and say he is driving. He never asked me to join him for a business lunch, but I just figured they were closer and it is clear he likes her. Lately, I have heard Les ask Amy to meet him for drinks and dinner, and Amy would refuse."

Joe said he has watched the two of them lately and Amy seems to try to keep her distance and will stand behind Joe's desk when she sees Les walking toward her. Joe had no recollection of a meeting of February 5th between Les and Amy.

Joe asked if Les will know what was said during this interview. I told him that his comments are confidential, and Les will not be told any information about what was said.

The meeting started at 2:00 pm on February 20th and ended at 2:25 pm.

I have read the above summary and it is true, accurate, and complete.

Dated: 02/20/2019   Signature: _____Joe Smith_____

                                                                                    Joe Smith

Summary Prepared by Josh Peters

Interview of Mary Johnson

Mary Johnson came to my (Josh Peters) office on February 20, 2019. She was hesitant to discuss the situation because she said she really does not like being involved in what she called, "office gossip" and besides, she didn't run for help when she was having issues. "I am a big girl, I took care of this stuff myself."

I asked her if she was aware of any questionable interactions between Amy and Les that struck her as unusual. "Here's the point, the only thing unusual is that you guys find his actions surprising. This is Les. He asked me to go dancing with him, he asked me to have drinks, and he asked me if I am lesbian. I told him if he ever hits on me again, I will make sure it is the last thing he ever does. He has not bothered me since."

Mary would not provide any more details of her interaction except to say some people run for help but that is not her way.

"I have seen Les move in on Amy like he used to on me. Amy seemed unsure of what to do. When he would go to hug her, she would just kind of fold up in his arms passively. She needs to be assertive and knee him in the you-know-whats. That would stop him from bothering her, but he would likely move on the next victim."

Mary said she told Amy she should stand her ground, but she was worried he could make her job horrible. Mary emphasized that every business has a guy like Les, and the trick is to let them know to buzz off.

The meeting began at 4:10 pm on February 20th and ended at 4:30 pm.

I have read the above summary and it is true, accurate, and complete.

Dated: 02/20/2019

Signature: _____*Mary Johnson*_____

Mary Johnson

Summary Prepared by Josh Peters

Evaluation and Response Report RE: Complaint against Les S. Moore

Prepared by: Josh Peters   Date of Report: February 22, 2019

Re: **Complaint against Les S. Moore**

This matter stems from an employee complaint brought by Amy Phafoofnik alleging inappropriate conduct by Les S. Moore. The specifics of her complaint are set forth in her signed written statement attached hereto as Attachment "A" from the February 15, 2019 interview.

Ms. Phafoofnik alleges that Les S. Moore has repeatedly asked her out over the course of the last 3 months. Amy stated Les also continually tries to hug her. She said on February 5th in his office Les told her he thinks about her when he is lying in bed. She also claims he inappropriately touched her shoulder when describing how he thinks of her while he is in his bed.

An investigation was initiated subsequent to the above referenced complaint. A meeting with the CIDER supervisor, Betsy Flannigan, and Josh Peters, was held on February 16, 2019 in Ms. Flannigan's office to discuss the scope of the investigation. A summary of that meeting is attached hereto as Attachment "B."

The investigation consisted of interviewing the following witnesses:

- Les S. Moore, the alleged harasser; his signed statement of February 17, 2019 is attached hereto as Attachment "C."
- Mary Johnson (set forth her position and department), her signed statement of February 20, 2019, is attached hereto as Attachment "D."
- Joe Smith (set forth his position and department), his signed statement of February 20, 2019, is attached hereto as Attachment "E."
- Kim Robertson (set forth her position and department), her signed statement of February 20, 2019, is attached hereto as Attachment "F."

Issues Raised: (Set forth each issue that was recognized by the company stemming from the complaint and subsequent investigation.)

  —*Complaint of Sexual Harassment against Les S. Moore brought by Amy P. & Mary Johnson.*

Findings: {Outline what the company discovered from the investigation. Differentiate between undisputed facts and areas in dispute or controversy. Do not confuse facts with opinions.

- On February 5, 2019, Les asked Amy to come to his office. Amy came in and sat down.
- Amy said Les put his hand on her shoulder in what she perceived as a sexual manner.
- Les said Amy was wearing a shirt that was inappropriate for work and he was demonstrating how her blouse dips down on her shoulder exposing her skin.
- Amy said Les told her he thinks of her while he is lying in bed.

- Les contested this and said he told her he was thinking of her before work regarding her inappropriate work attire and never mentioned anything about bed.
- Les emphasized what he perceived is new movement in the company where women are blindly believed and whatever a man says is discounted.
- The witnesses corroborate Amy's perspective. Further, Mary revealed that Les behaved inappropriately toward her in the past. She said she did not report his misconduct.
- Les has had a previous complaint against him for sexual harassment. He was given a warning and was sent to a two-day sensitivity training to help overcome this problem.

Evaluation: The CIDER supervisor, Betsy, reviewed the investigation including the witness statements and phone recording of one hug between Amy P. and Les M. and analysis of all the material and a discussion that included the investigator's (Josh P's) opinions regarding plausibility and demeanor of all witnesses. It was determined that none of the witnesses had any motive to falsify their account. While Les has denied Amy's allegations, the weight of the evidence supports the determination that Les S. Moore sexually harassed an employee. In addition, there is evidence of Les sexually harassing Mary Johnson. Consequently, immediate action must be taken.

Responses considered: Additional sensitivity training for Mr. Moore; demoting Mr. Moore to a non-supervisory position; suspending him without pay; transferring Ms. Phafoofnik so she is not under Mr. Moore's authority; terminating Mr. Moore. It is clear the sensitivity training did not remedy the problem. Keeping on Mr. Moore in the company will likely lead to additional issues.

Response(s) selected: The company has determined that the appropriate response is to fire Les S. Moore immediately. Betsy will fire him at the conclusion of the work day today (February 22, 2019). Mr. Moore is an At-Will employee; consequently, there is no issue with an immediate termination. Betsy will prepare a brief written statement to give to Mr. Moore outlining the reason for termination.

Ed Jones, the company vice-president, will be a part of the termination process. Human resources will be contacted to prepare a check for salary and vacation time owed and also to provide him with COBRA information. Josh will meet with Amy to review the company's response. A staff meeting will be held tomorrow (February 23rd) to discuss the personnel changes. Betsy will follow the company's termination checklist, and prepare a written account of the termination meeting to properly document the file.

Dated: 02/22/2019   Signature of person preparing the report: _____*Josh Peters*_____

Josh Peters

(Signature of Supervisor and date) ___*Betsy Flannigan*___ 02/22/2019